ESSENTIAL
EMPLOYMENT
LAW

Cavendish
Publishing
Limited

London • Sydney

Titles in the series:

ESSENTIAL EMPLOYMENT LAW

Marnah Suff, BA, LLB, Cert F Ed, Barrister

Cavendish
Publishing
Limited

London • Sydney

First published in Great Britain 1998 by Cavendish Publishing Limited, The Glass House, Wharton Street, London WC1X 9PX

Telephone: 0171-278 8000   Facsimile: 0171-278 8080

e-mail: info@cavendishpublishing.com

Visit our Home Page on http://www.cavendishpublishing.com

Suff, Marnah

Essential employment law

1. Labour laws and legislation – Great Britain

I. Title II. Employment law

344.4'1'01

ISBN 1 85941 367 6

Printed and bound in Great Britain

Foreword

This book is part of the Cavendish Essential series. The books in the series are designed to provide useful revision aids for the hard-pressed student. They are not, of course, intended to be substitutes for more detailed treatises. Other textbooks in the Cavendish portfolio must supply these gaps.

The Cavendish Essential series is now in its second edition and is a well-established favourite among students.

The team of authors bring a wealth of lecturing and examining experience to the task in hand. Many of us can even recall what it was like to face law examinations!

Professor Nicholas Bourne
General Editor, Essential Series
Swansea
Summer 1997

Acknowledgments

I wish to thank my colleagues and my students for their guidance and advice in planning this book, and Mrs Maureen Turner for her invaluable assistance with the word processing.

Preface

This book is intended as a revision aid for students studying for degree and other examinations in employment law.

Since employment law has grown enormously in recent years and space is limited, this book concentrates on the essential content of employment law – the relationship between an employer and his employees and trade unions; the regulations on health and safety at work, and the governance of trade unions are not included.

Reference will also have to be made to other volumes for the historical development of the law, its political significance and industrial relations implications.

Marnah Suff
October 1997

Preface

Contents

1 Introduction

You should be familiar with the following areas:

- the scope of employment law
- the sources of employment law including European law
- the machinery for resolving disputes in employment
- statutory bodies with specialised employment functions

The scope of employment law

Employment law is one of the more dynamic and controversial areas of English law; so controversial, in fact, that there is no agreement even on what it should be called. Books headed Labour Law, Employment Law or Industrial Law, will be found to cover much the same material, ie:

- individual employment law – the law governing the relationship between individual employees and their employer;
- collective labour law – the law governing the relationship between employers and employee organisations, ie – trade unions;
- statutory controls over health and safety at work.

Due to the major growth in the content of employment law generally, the law on health and safety at work often has to be moved to a separate manual. The law on health and safety at work is not covered in this volume.

Employment law is a matter of close interest to political parties, which accounts for the growth of legislation on employment matters in the last 30 years. It is also a matter of concern for the European

Union, and there has been a vast influx of law from Europe into UK employment law in recent years, not all of it tune with the views of the government of the day.

It is necessary to consider briefly the sources of employment law and the legal framework within which it operates.

Sources of employment law

Labour law is found in common law, in statute law, and in European law.

Common law

The relationship of employer and employee, the terms of the contracts of employment, the respective duties of employer and employee are all governed by the principles of the law of contract which emanate from the common law. In addition, access to the statutory protection given to employees is dependent on the existence of the contract of employment whose requirements are again set by the common law.

The common law has also been important in the development of collective labour law. Trade unions were illegal organisations in the eyes of the common law and any industrial action they organised was seen as a civil offence, ie a tort. Statutory protection has been given to both trade unions and their activities over the years. It is still necessary, however, in any action to restrain trade union activity to first identify the tort they are alleged to be committing. The common law also remains important in establishing the relationship between a trade union and its members.

Legislation

Legislation has become increasingly important in recent years. In the 1960s and 1970s many Acts of Parliament provided new rights for employees, eg the right to redundancy payments, the right not to be unfairly dismissed, the right not to be discriminated against on the ground of sex or race. In the 1980s and 1990s, the emphasis changed with the advent of the Conservative government and much legislation was introduced to restrict the immunities of trade unions organising industrial action. It will be interesting to note what developments will take place under the new Labour government.

European Law

Entry into the European Union has resulted in very many significant developments. European law takes precedence over national law, whether case law, prior legislation or even subsequent legislation (*Factortame v Secretary of State for Transport* (1991)).

The greatest effect on English law has been in the area of sex discrimination, transfer of undertakings and health and safety. It can be expected to have even greater impact in the future with the advent of a Labour government and its proposed adherence to the Social Chapter.

There are three basic sources of European law.

The Treaty of Rome

The Treaty of Rome is directly effective within all the countries of the European Union, and does not need any national legislation for its implementation. It has direct effect both horizontally and vertically, that is to say it will confer rights upon individuals both against other private citizens and against the state, eg s 119 of the Treaty of Rome which requires equal pay for men and women (see Chapter 4).

The legislation of the European Union

* Regulations, which like the Treaty are directly applicable; and
* Directives, which require national governments to introduce legislation to achieve a certain end. If not implemented, or imperfectly implemented, these too can be directly effective in so far as they affect 'emanations of the state' (ie vertical effect). This phrase has been liberally interpreted to cover not only public authorities but 'a body, whatever its form which has been made responsible, pursuant to a method adopted by the state, for providing a public service under the control of the state'. On this basis, the House of Lords held that British Gas was an emanation of the state (*Foster v British Gas* (1991)).

They are not, however, directly effective against private employers (they do not have horizontal effect). Employees of private employers may instead sue the government for damages for their failure to implement the directive as required. In *Francovich v Italian Republic* (1992), it was held that a government could be sued provided:

  – the directive was intended to confer rights on individuals;

  – it is sufficiently clear and direct;

3

– the individual can show that he suffered loss as a result of the government's failure.

In the early years, directives could only be passed by the unanimous vote of all Member States, but in 1986 the Single European Act permitted majority voting on measures aimed at the functioning of the internal market. While unanimity is still required with regard to general employment law matters, qualified majority voting applies to directives on health and safety. It is expected, with the growth in the numbers of countries within the European Union, that qualified majority voting will increase.

The Social Chapter

In Maastricht in 1989, the UK vetoed an attempt by the other states to incorporate a Community Charter on the Social Rights of Workers into the Treaty of Rome. The other members then agreed to add a Protocol to the Treaty which allowed them to use the Community institutions to issue directives which applied to them but not to the UK. In the Council of Ministers, qualified voting and unanimous voting will take place as if the UK were not a member. Two directives have so far been issued – a Directive on European Works Councils (Chapter 10) and a Directive on Parental Leave (Chapter 3).

The Labour government has announced its intention to accede to the Social Chapter and these directives, and others to be issued under this heading, will eventually apply to the UK. The timescale for implementing the existing directives is not yet clear

The decisions of the European Court of Justice (ECJ)

The ECJ is the final arbiter in the interpretation of European law. When matters involving European law arise in a case, they can be referred directly to the ECJ for resolution or they can be decided by the national court in accordance with existing interpretations of the European Court.

Examples of the methods by which European law influences UK employment law

• Legislative implementation

The Transfer of Undertakings Regulations (TUPE) 1981 were introduced in order to comply with the Acquired Rights Directive 77/18.7 (see Chapter 3).

Changes were made in TURERA 1993 to written particulars, unfair dismissal and pregnancy protection in accordance with various directives (see Chapters 2, 3 and 7).

Changes were made to the Equal Pay Act in 1983, and to the Sex Discrimination Act in 1986, in order to comply with decisions of the ECJ (see Chapter 4).

- Judicial implementation – direct effect

  The European Community Act 1972 accepted that EC law should be enforced in the UK, therefore:

  (a) National courts are under a duty not to apply UK law which conflicts with EU law, eg *Webb v EMO Cargo (UK)* (1994) (see Chapter 4).

  (b) The Treaty of Rome confers rights on individuals providing it is unconditional and sufficiently precise: *Barber v Guardian Royal Exchange Assurance Group* (1994) (see Chapter 4).

  (c) Directives (again if unconditional and sufficiently precise) are directly effective against 'emanations of the state', eg *Foster v British Gas* (1991).

- Judicial implementation – indirect effect

  Uniform principles of interpretation are to be applied throughout the Union. The 'purposive' European approach to interpretation should be applied to both directives and corresponding UK legislation. In *Marleasing* it was held that UK legislation should be interpreted in accordance with the relevant directive irrespective of whether the legislation was introduced in order to implement the directive, eg in *Pickstone v Freemans* (1988) words were implied into the Equal Pay Act in order to make it comply with s 119 (see Chapter 4).

- Judicial review

  (a) Subordinate legislation, eg regulations, may be challenged on the ground that it is *ultra vires*, eg the 'commercial venture' requirement in TUPE (see Chapter 3);

  (b) Primary legislation, ie Acts of Parliament may be challenged if it conflicts with EU Law, eg *R v Secretary of State for Employment, ex p EOC* (1994) which led to the abandonment of the minimum hours per week requirement for unfair dismissal and redundancy payments.

- Infringement proceedings

  Infringement proceeding were brought against the UK government in respect of their failure to implement properly the provisions of s 119 of the Equal Pay Act 1983, the Sex Discrimination Act 1986 and the requirements of the Acquired Rights Directive in TUPE.

- Damages against the government

  See *Francovich v Italian Govt* (1992) above, p 3.

The machinery for resolving disputes

The institutions of employment law reflect to a large extent the sources of employment law.

Civil courts

Disputes arising in connection with common law matters are mainly dealt with in the ordinary courts, eg purely contractual matters are dealt with in the county court or the High Court according to the amounts of money involved. Applications for an injunction to stop a union proceeding with industrial action will again be heard in the High Court, as will a complaint by a union member that the union has not complied with its own rules or has infringed the rules of natural justice in its dealings with him.

However, following the mass of legislation introduced in the last 30 years, many new institutions have been created to deal specifically with employment and industrial relations disputes.

Industrial tribunals

Industrial tribunals were established originally by the Industrial Training Act 1964 to deal with disputes arising from that Act, but their jurisdiction has extended considerably since that time. They are now governed by the Industrial Tribunal Act 1996.

Composition and procedure

The tribunals are organised on a regional basis, and each tribunal consists of a legally-qualified chairman and two lay members, one drawn from a panel nominated by employers' organisations, and the other from a panel nominated by employee organisations.

Legal aid is not available for industrial tribunals. Proceedings are intended to be less formal, less expensive and speedier than that of a court. Originally it was believed that persons would appear themselves without the need for legal representation. However, in recent years, tribunals have become more legalistic, and legal, or other representation is more common and seems especially desirable in claims involving complicated matters of law such as equal pay, discrimination, reductions in wages or the transfer of an undertaking.

Costs are not normally awarded but may be ordered if one of the parties has behaved 'frivolously, vexatiously, or otherwise unreasonably'.

A tribunal may order a *prehearing review*, on the application of one party or on its own motion, where it appears that some contention is unlikely to succeed. This may be conducted by the Chairman alone; written or oral representations may be made but no witnesses will be called, nor documents considered. If the tribunal decides that the contention is a hopeless one, then it can require the party concerned to deposit £150 if he or she insists on continuing the proceedings.

The chairman may sit alone to consider cases on reductions in wages, cases in contract, and cases where both parties consent to his doing so.

Tribunals may review their own decision within 14 days of the decision being sent out, on the grounds that:

- there was an error by tribunal staff;
- one party did not receive notice of the hearing;
- the decision was made in the absence of one of the parties;
- new evidence has become available; or
- the interests of justice requires such a review.

There is a right of appeal to the Employment Appeal Tribunal within six weeks on a point of law.

Jurisdiction

Industrial tribunals are empowered to deal with a wide range of matters arising from a number of statutory provisions. The most important of which regard complaints concerning:

- the written particulars of the terms of employment;
- redundancy payments;
- unfair dismissal;
- guarantee payments;
- suspension from work on medical grounds;

- trade union membership and activities;
- time off work;
- the right to maternity leave;
- The Sex Discrimination Act;
- The Equal Pay Act;
- The Race Relations Act;
- time off for ante-natal care;
- secret ballots;
- unreasonable exclusion from trade union membership;
- failure to consult a trade union on redundancies or the transfer of an undertaking; or
- unlawful refusal of employment on the grounds of trade union membership.

They now also have jurisdiction over contractual claims which:

- arise or are outstanding on the termination of an employee's employment;
- are not greater than £25,000;
- are brought within three months of the termination of employment;
- do not relate to personal injuries, living accommodation, intellectual property, breach of confidence, restrictive covenants.

The employer may bring a counterclaim within six weeks.

The Employment Appeal Tribunal

The Employment Appeal Tribunal (EAT) was originally set up by the Employment Protection Act 1975. It consists of a chairman who is a High Court judge and two or four lay members chosen as for the industrial tribunal.

It hears appeals on points of law only from the industrial tribunal on most of the jurisdictions exercised by a tribunal and from the Certification Officer. Appeals are restricted to points of law in order to discourage appeals. In *BT v Sheridan* (1990) it was stated by the Court of Appeal that points of law cover only:

- an error of law; and
- the tribunal's decision was perverse.

The EAT is not bound by its own previous decisions.

Appeals from the EAT lie to the Court of Appeal and thence to the House of Lords. If the case has a European dimension, it may be referred to the ECJ.

Advisory, Conciliation and Arbitration Service (ACAS)

ACAS was set up in the mid-1970s to improve industrial relations and and to encourage collective bargaining. The latter function, however, has been taken away and ACAS now aids the settlement of industrial disputes. It is regulated by TULR(C)A 1992 as amended by TURERA 1993.

ACAS has a tripartite structure which is common in employment situations. Three members are independent, three represent employers and three represent employees. The chairman is appointed by the government, but the government cannot direct ACAS as to how to exercise its function. ACAS may charge fees to those persons who benefit from its activity; however, fees are charged at present only for certain publications and seminars.

The functions of ACAS reflect its name, and are as follows:

- Advice

  It provides free advice on a wide range of employment matters to both employers and employees. Some 40,000 queries a year are usually dealt with.

- Conciliation

  (a) Individual disputes – Every application to an industrial tribunal is referred to ACAS who try to effect an agreement between the parties without the need for a hearing. It is estimated that one-third of claims are settled at this stage, and another one-third are withdrawn. With one exception only, an agreement to settle an industrial tribunal complaint will only be binding if it has been effected through ACAS. The one exception relates to a settlement agreed by the claimant's legally-qualified advisor.

  (b) Collective disputes – ACAS may strive to bring disputing parties together in order to reach a settlement either on its own initiative or at the request of one of the parties.

- Arbitration

  Where a trade dispute exists, ACAS may, with the consent of the parties, refer the matter to an independent arbitrator or to the

Central Arbitration Committee (CAC).

- Codes of Practice

ACAS is empowered to issue Codes of Practice 'containing such practical guidance as the service thinks fit for the purpose of promoting the improvement of industrial relations'. Codes of Practice have been issued on Disciplinary Practices and Procedures in Employment; Disclosure of Information to Trade Unions for Collective Bargaining Purposes; and Time Off for Trade Union Duties and Activities. Also an advisory booklet on Discipline at Work. Codes of Practice are not legally binding in that failure to follow the Codes will not necessarily attract liability but they must be taken into account by the industrial tribunals whenever relevant.

The Central Arbitration Committee (CAC)

This was set up in 1975 as a permanent and independent industrial relations arbitration body and is now governed by TULR(C)A 1992. It consists of a chairman and representatives of employers and employees. There are a number of deputy chairmen who share the work. Arbitration committees are set up with a chairman and an equal number of members from both sides of industry.

Their function is to hear complaints from trade unions that an employer has failed to disclose information for collective bargaining purposes (see Chapter 10). If an employer fails to comply with a declaration of the CAC, then it may declare that certain terms should automatically become part of the contract of employment of the relevant employee. This is a compulsory arbitration power.

The CAC will also arbitrate on disputes referred to it by ACAS. This is a voluntary power.

Before 1980 it also had compulsory powers to arbitrate in recognition disputes. This was abolished in 1980, but the Labour government have indicated that they will bring back compulsory recognition procedure. There is no appeal from the decisions of the CAC, but they may be challenged by judicial review proceedings in the High Court.

Statutory bodies with specific functions

The Certification Officer

The office of Certification Officer was created in 1975 to:

- maintain a list of independent trade unions; and
- to issue certificates of independence to trade unions.

Most rights given to trade unions are given to independent trade unions, so a certificate of independence is a vital matter (see Chapter 10).

Additional duties have been entrusted to the Certification Officer since 1979. The Officer also:

- keeps records of annual membership and financial returns, copies of union rules and other documents which unions are required to file;
- investigates complaints concerning the election of trade union officials, the allotting procedures for setting-up political funds, political expenditure and the amalgamation of trade unions.

An annual report is made to the Secretary of State for Employment who will present it to Parliament.

Commissioner for the Rights of Trade Union Members (CROTUM)

This office was created by the Employment Act 1980, now s 266 of the TULR(C)A 1992, to assist union members in taking action against their own union where the latter has:

- failed to comply with the regulations on political expenditure, the election of union officials, the use of funds or property, ballots for industrial action and maintenance of the register of members;
- taken disciplinary or expulsion proceedings against a member.

The assistance includes funding the cost of legal advice and representation.

Commissioner for Protection Against Unlawful Industrial Action (COPAUIA)

This office was created in 1993 – now s 235B of the TULR(C)A 1992.

The Commissioner has the power to assist any party who wishes to take action on the basis that the supply of goods or services to him or her has been prevented or delayed by unlawful industrial action. Such assistance may take the form of financial assistance for legal advice or representation or in the form of an indemnity in respect of costs.

The Commissions

Commissions have been set up to oversee and assist in the operation of various legislation.

The Equal Opportunities Commission (EOC)

The EOC was established by the Sex Discrimination Act in 1975. It consists of between eight and 15 members. It has a duty to:

- work towards eliminating discrimination on the grounds of sex;
- promote equality of opportunity between men and women;
- review the operation of the Sex Discrimination Act 1986 and the Equal Pay Act 1983; and
- submit proposals for amendment.

It has the power to:

- give advice and financial support to suitable claimants;
- take action itself in respect of certain acts, eg advertisements;
- formulate and issues Codes of Practice which have the same effect as ACAS Codes;
- carry out formal investigations, but only where it has some evidence that unlawful acts are taking place (*Re Prestige Group plc* (1984));
- where it discovers discrimination, to issue non-discriminatory notices.

The Commission for Racial Equality

The Commission for Racial Equality (CRE) was established by the Race Relations Act 1976. Its remit and powers are very similar to those of the EOC above. It has a duty to:

- work towards the elimination of discrimination;
- promote equality of opportunity and good relations between persons of different racial groups;
- keep under review the working of the Act.

It has, however, a wider jurisdiction with regard to non-employment matters.

2 The contract of employment

You should be familiar with the following areas:

- the distinction between contracts of employment and self-employment
- the formation and variation of a contract of employment
- the terms agreed between employer and employee, whether express or implied
- the terms implied by the common law
- the terms incorporated from collective agreements, awards or otherwise

Steven Anderman has pointed out that the contract of employment is central to British labour law.

- Many statutory rights – eg unfair dismissal, redundancy payments – are dependent on the presence of a contract of employment. In addition, common law contractual concepts are used to define certain elements of the statutory rights.
- There is no legal structure for collective agreements. They become enforceable only when incorporated into an individual contract of employment.
- The economic torts which are the basis for controlling industrial action are based on a breach of the contract of employment.
- The contract itself is an important source of employment rights and duties, both in respect of express terms – eg salaries, hours of work holidays – and terms implied by the court.

The contract of employment and self-employment

Despite its pivotal role, there is no statutory definition of a contract of employment. It can, in some circumstances, be difficult to distinguish between a contract of service (a contract of employment) and a contract for service (self-employment). In view of the importance of this distinction, it is unfortunate that there is a lack of precision in the dividing line between them.

Significance of the distinction

1   Only an employee qualifies for:
    • Employment rights granted under the Employment Rights Act 1996, eg guarantee payments, entitlement to written particulars, protection against unfair dismissal, redundancy payments, minimum periods of notice and so on.
    • Certain social security benefits such as unemployment benefit.
    • Certain health and safety protection, eg under the Factories Act.
    • The benefit of certain implied terms, eg the employers duty of care.
2   An important distinction concerns taxation. Employees are taxed under Schedule E of the Income and Corporation Taxes Act 1970, whilst the self-employed enjoy more favourable treatment, being taxed under Schedule D, with more generous allowances.
3   An employer is vicariously liable for all the torts committed by his employees, but is not normally responsible for the torts of his independent contractors.

From the employer's point of view, it may be desirable to hire independent contractors, as witnessed by the growth of self-employment in recent years. The employer is relieved of the administrative tasks involved in making PAYE deductions and National Insurance deductions from wages. It may have certain VAT advantages and help to avoid the need to negotiate with trade unions. It also frees him or her from having to observe the provisions of the Employment Rights Act 1996.

Advantages to the individual employee, however, tend to be more apparent than real. He must ensure that he is paid enough to cover insurance premiums, holiday money, pension contributions. Most of the industrial safety legislation, some of the most important social security rights, and the modern employment protection legislation apply only to employed persons. According to Smith and Wood, 'An independent contractor may be in a better monetary position while working, but at a grave disadvantage if he falls off a ladder or is sacked'.

Identifying the contract of employment

The control test
In Victorian times, the distinguishing element was control. In *Yewens v Noakes* (1880) it was stated that 'A servant is a person subject to the command of his master as to the manner in which he shall do his work'. Today control is still important: but it is not decisive. It is inappropriate, for instance, when dealing with persons with special skills.

The organisation test
The control test was briefly replaced by the organisation test which required an employee to be an integral part of the employer's organisation. In *Cassidy v Ministry of Health* (1951) it was held that the Ministry was vicariously liable for the negligence of a surgeon in performing an operation because the hospital authority was in a position to make rules concerning the organisation of the medical staff's work, as opposed to the manner in which it was done. The surgeon was an integral part of the organisation. The great disadvantage of this approach lies in its failure to define exactly what is meant by integration and organisation.

The multiple test
The modern approach has been to abandon the search for a single test and to adopt a multiple test, thereby weighing all the factors for and against the existence of a contract of employment to decide whether a worker is in business on his own account. Control and organisation are taken into account, as is the power to suspend and dismiss, and pensions; but no one factor is decisive. In *Ready Mixed Concrete v Ministry of Pensions* (1968), McKenna J held that there were three conditions necessary to establish that a contract of service existed:

- the employee agreed to provide his own work and skill;
- there must be some element of control exercised by the employer;
- the other terms of the contract must not be inconsistent with the existence of a contract of employment.

In *Market Investigations Ltd v Minister of Social Security* (1969), an inter-viewer worked infrequently under a series of contracts whereby she interviewed in accordance with the company's instructions. She had to complete the work within a certain time but otherwise had no speci-fied hours of work. There was no provision for holiday or sick pay and she was free to work for other organisations. The court found that the company did have some control over the way in which she worked, and that the terms of the contract were consistent with a contract of service. She did not provide any equipment and took no risks. The court concluded *she was not in business on her own account*. The court emphasised that there was 'no exhaustive test compiled nor strict rules laid down' but suggested that the following would be among the fac-tors to be considered:

- degree of control by the employer;
- degree to which the worker risks loss/stands to profit;
- ownership of tools and equipment;
- degree to which the worker is an integral part of the business;
- method of payment;
- whether deductions are made for tax and national insurance;
- whether there is a mutuality of obligation;
- the terms used by the parties – a factor to be considered but not decisive.

In *Lee v Chung and Shun Shing Construction Group* (1990), the Privy Council implicitly approved of the test of 'Is he in business on his own account?' and also the criteria adopted in *Market Investigations* (above).

A decision for the courts

The label given to the arrangement by the parties themselves will be taken into consideration but, as stated above, it is not decisive. The court will look at the essence of the arrangement, not merely at any agree-ment between the parties themselves as to how it should be treated.

In *Ferguson v John Dawson & Partners* (1976), Ferguson worked as a labourer on a building site. He was designated as a labour-only sub-contractor. The Court of Appeal held that he was an employee; his work was under the control of the firm's site manager. The court stat-ed that it considered the concept of the 'lump' (labour-only subcon-tracting) as being no more than a device which each party regarded as being capable of being put to his own advantage, but which in reality did not affect the relationship of the parties. Control was the dominant factor in this case.

In *Lane v Shire Roofing Co Ltd* (1995), the Court of Appeal agreed that control was an important element but stated that it might not be relevant in the case of a skilled worker with discretion to decide how the work should be carried out. In such cases the test should be 'Whose business was it?' Was the worker carrying out his own business or was he working on his employer's business? The Court of Appeal held that a builder who ran his own one-man business and who was categorised as self-employed for tax purposes was an employee when he was employed by a roofing firm to re-roof a porch, injuring himself badly whilst doing so. They went on to say that in the case of safety at work there was a real public interest in recognising an employer/employee relationship where it existed, because of the statutory and common law duties placed on the employer.

The Court of Appeal stated in *Massey v Crown Life Insurance Co Ltd* (1978) that where the nature of the relationship is in doubt or is ambiguous, the label given to the relationship by the parties themselves could solve the ambiguity. In that case, the court accepted that a branch manager who had arranged to be treated as self-employed and registered himself as John Massey & Associates was an independent contractor. However, in *Young & Woods v West* (1980), where a sheet-metal worker chose to be treated as self-employed, the Court of Appeal stated that it was impossible to regard Woods as being in business on his own account, and he was therefore held to be an employee. The court stated that the label chosen by the parties can be a relevant factor but only if other factors did not dictate a different answer.

In the above cases, the most important factors are seen to be 'control' and the 'own business' test.

Atypical workers

Another test which has become important, particularly in relation to 'peripheral workers' or atypical workers, is mutuality of obligation.

In *O'Kelly v Trusthouse Forte Plc* (1983), the Court of Appeal refused to find regular casual waiters were employees even though they had a well-established and regular working relationship with Trusthouse Forte. It was held that the relationship lacked the essential mutuality of obligation to classify them as employees. The company had no obligation to offer them work and technically the workers could refuse work when it was offered even though in practice they did not do so, because refusal would result in removal from the regular list.

The same reasoning is also found in *Wickens v Campion Employment* (1984), where 'temps' engaged by a private employment agency were not accorded employment status because of the lack of a binding obligation on the part of the agency to make bookings for work, and the absence of any obligation on the part of the typists to accept any bookings made. Similarly, in *McLeod v Hellyer* (1987), the court found that trawlermen who entered into separate contracts for each voyage were self-employed.

A different approach was taken by the court in *Nethermere (St Neots) Ltd v Gardiner* (1983). Here homeworkers making clothing were accorded employee status on the basis that the regular giving and taking of work over a period evidenced the necessary mutuality of obligation. This was held to be so even though the workers were under no obligation to undertake a particular quantity of work and in certain weeks did no work at all.

It has been suggested that because atypical workers are now becoming almost typical the courts should take this into account.

In *Clark v Oxfordshire Health Authority* (1996), a nurse who was retained by a health authority on a casual basis to fill temporary vacancies was held to be an employee. The Employment Appeal Tribunal (EAT) stated that the nature of employment has changed in recent years and that many employees are expected to be more flexible in their working arrangements.

In *City and East London FHS Authority v Durcan* (1996), the EAT upheld a decision that a dentist who was employed for one evening a week at a local hospital was an employee.

Secondment of employees

Where an employee is seconded to another firm, his original firm will remain liable unless it can be proved that control was transferred.

In *Mersey Docks and Harbour Board v Coggin and Griffiths* (1947), the Harbour Board loaned a crane and a driver to a firm of stevedores who became responsible for the driver's wages. It was held that the Harbour Board were the driver's employers as they had failed to prove that control had been transferred. Conversely, in *Garrard v Southey* (1952), the plaintiff was loaned to carry out some electrical work. The foreman of the temporary employers not only told him what to do but also specifically controlled the way he was to do it. It was held that the temporary employers were his employer in the circumstances.

The court distinguished between cases where a complicated piece of equipment was loaned together with an employee and where an unskilled or semi-skilled workman was transferred on his own. Transfer of employment is more easily accepted in the latter case.

Agency workers

The above rules are applied. Although the Employment Agencies Act 1976 requires agencies to communicate to their clients and workers the status of the latter, this is not conclusive since the courts may have regard to the real relationship. Depending on the actual arrangements, an agency worker may be self-employed, an employee of the client, or an employee of the agency.

In *McMeechan v Secretary of State for Employment* (1995), the Court of Appeal held that an agency worker had a contract of employment despite the fact that his contract of service described him as self-employed. The court stated that the status of the employee depended on the interpretation of all the terms of the contract. Matters which led to the decision included the agency's right to dismiss, a grievance procedure and the duty of confidentiality.

Directors

General rule – a non-executive director will not be an employee: an executive director may be an employee. However, in *Buchan v Secretary of State for Employment* (1996) and *Ivey v Secretary of State for Employment* (1996), two company directors who owned controlling interests in their companies were held by the EAT not to be employees. It was stated that it would, for instance, be inappropriate to allow such individuals to claim unfair dismissal or redundancy payments since the decision to dismiss them could only have been taken with their consent.

Partners

Partners are self-employed.

Law and fact

The Privy Council confirmed in *Lee v Chung* (1990) the statement made by the Court of Appeal in *O'Kelly v Trusthouse Forte* (1983) that the categorisation of the contract is a question of fact, not a question of law, apart from those cases where the tribunal is required to interpret a written document, as in *Davies v Presbyterian Council of Wales* (1986).

As an appeal can only be made on a question of law, or on the ground that the decision of the tribunal is perverse, few appeals can be made. It has been pointed out by Pitt that this could result in different tribunals reaching different conclusions on very similar facts.

Rideout states that this century has produced a test which has now been realised not to be a test (the organisation test) and has also embarked upon a long search for a substitute test (multiple test). The distinction between employed and self-employed has become genuinely fluid and difficult to draw a line under.

It is sometimes suggested that the distinction between employment and self-employment should be differently drawn according to the purpose for which it is being made, so that, for instance, one might lean more heavily in favour of employment status in unfair dismissal case and industrial safety cases than in tax and social security cases. Davies and Friedland, however, consider that this fragmentation according to the nature of the proceedings would discredit the claim of the process of definition to be an objective test, such a claim being necessary, in their opinion, to give internal strength to the distinction.

The courts have experienced great difficulty in classifying so-called 'peripheral' or 'atypical' workers – those whose work is temporary, part-time or casual. Given that, at present, they make up an estimated one-third of the labour force and that their numbers are increasing, it has been argued that employment protection legislation should be extended to cover this group of workers, as is already the case with regard to anti-discrimination law.

Formation of the contract

A contract of employment can be entered into formally or informally. It can emerge as a result of an advertisement, an interview, negotiations, exchange of letters or casual conversations.

To be a valid contract it will require an offer and an acceptance of that offer; an intention to be legally bound, certainty of terms and consideration. Its validity can be affected by illegality, lack of capacity, misrepresentation, mistake, duress or undue influence.

Job advertisements do not normally amount to an offer but can be used to help interpret the contract.

Illegality

In practice, illegality provides the main problem. If a contract is illegal at common law, this will render void not only the agreed and incorporated terms but also the terms implied by common law or imposed by legislation. A contract is void for illegality if it is for an illegal purpose, eg to defraud the inland revenue.

In *Cole v Fred Stacey* (1974), the employee was given an additional payment which was not taxed as income. It was held that he was not entitled to a redundancy payment as the contract was illegal and void.

Not knowing that an action is illegal will not validate the contract. In *Salveson v Simons* (1994), a farm manager had most of his salary paid under the PAYE system, but £2,000 was paid as management fees to a partnership of which he was a member but which carried out no identifiable services. The EAT maintained that this was clearly a case of defrauding the inland revenue; the fact that the parties did not realise that it was illegal was irrelevant and the contract was void. The claimant could not therefore sue for unfair dismissal.

A contract will not be void, however, against an employee:

- if the illegality was only in its performance, eg a driver was convicted of exceeding the speed limit during the course of his employment;
- if the employee was unaware of the illegality and did not profit from it, eg *Hewcastle Catering v Ahmed* (1991): two employees were allowed to sue for unfair dismissal although they had carried out their employer's instructions to present bills in a way which could allow the employer to evade making VAT payments.

The written statement of terms

Section 1 of the Employment Rights Act 1996 requires an employer to give employees a written statement of certain terms and conditions of their employment within eight weeks of the commencement of employment. The aim of this provision is to ensure that the employee knows his legal rights under the contract. The statement need not be given to the self-employed, employees who work mainly outside the UK and employees who work for less than eight hours a week.

The statement must contain the following information:

- identification of the parties;
- the date on which employment began and the date on which the employee's period of continuous service began, taking into account any employment with a previous employer which counts towards that period. (This is important for the employee to calculate his entitlement to many statutory benefits.)
- scale or rate of pay;
- intervals of pay – weekly, monthly, etc;
- hours of work;
- holiday entitlement (including statutory holidays) and holiday pay;
- job title, or brief description of work; and
- the place or places of work.

The above terms must be set out in one document, called the principle document. In addition, the following information must be given but may be given in instalments provided all information is given within an eight week period:

- sick leave and any entitlement to sick pay;
- pension and pension schemes – whether a contracting out certificate is in force;
- where the employment is not permanent, the period for which it is intended to continue, or the date on which it is to end;
- any collective agreement which affects the terms and conditions of employment;
- where the employee is expected to work outside the UK, the period of foreign service, the currency to be used for pay and any extra benefits.

In addition, if the employer has more than 20 employees, he must give them details of any disciplinary or grievance procedures, specifying the person to whom the employee may apply if he has a grievance or is dissatisfied with any disciplinary decision and any further steps which may follow.

Terms and conditions relating to absence for sickness or injury, or to pension schemes, or to disciplinary or grievance procedures need not be given in detail but may refer to another document which is reasonably accessible to the employee, eg a company handbook. Reference may be made to a collective agreement or to statutory rights in the case of length of notice.

Changes
Any changes in the terms contained in the written particulars must be communicated in writing to employees within one month of the change.

Status of the written statement
The written statement is not a contract of employment merely a statement of those terms of the contract required by law to be included in the written statement. As such:

- It is *prima facie*, but not conclusive evidence, of the terms of the contract. The employer can show that it is erroneous by bringing strong evidence to the contrary; the employee may challenge it on the basis of less strong evidence. In *System Floors v Daniel* (1982), an employee was able to show that the date of commencement of employment shown in the written particulars was incorrect. The fact that the employee did not challenge the statement when it is issued does not prevent him from challenging it at a later date. The signature of the employee only indicates receipt of the document. However if it is headed 'Contract of Employment' and is signed as such by an employee, then it will be taken to be the contract of employment, and the parol evidence rule will apply (*Gascol Conversions v Mercer* (1974)).

- It will not necessarily contain all the terms of the contract.

Remedy for failure to provide a written statement

An employee may apply to the industrial tribunal which may declare what particulars the employee should have been given. It was held in *Eagland v BT plc* (1993) that the tribunal may identify a term that has been agreed – either expressly, or by implication – from the surrounding circumstances or the behaviour of the parties, but it may not invent terms which had not been agreed by any of the above methods.

Terms agreed between employer and employee

Express terms

The express terms may be written, oral, or partly written and partly oral. The written parts may be found in various pieces of paper, including correspondence, works rules, collective agreements, staff handbooks or company journals. The task of the tribunal will be to interpret the meaning of such express terms.

In *Cole v Midland Display Ltd* (1973), the employee was a manager employed on a 'staff basis'. He refused to do overtime without pay and his subsequent dismissal was held to be fair. The essence of being employed on a staff basis at that time was that he was guaranteed wages whether there was work or not including during sickness. In return, 'staff' were expected to work overtime where necessary, without pay if reasonably requested to do so.

Although it may be possible to refer to an advertisement in order to ascertain the exact terms of a contract, such statements cannot override the express terms. In *Deeley v British Rail Engineering* (1980), the advertisement referred to a 'Sales Engineer (Export)'. The contract, however, referred to a 'Sales Engineer', and the written terms stated that he was to perform duties 'as required' by his employer. It was held that he was a 'Sales Engineer' and not an 'Export Sales Engineer'.

Implied terms

In addition to the express terms, there are terms which will be implied into the contract, in order to give 'business efficacy' to the contract (the *Moorcock* basis). Such terms are terms implied in fact and are based on the presumed intention of the parties. *Cf* terms implied in law, below.

The test used is that of the 'officious bystander' who on asking whether such and such a provision was part of the contract, would have been told 'of course, it was too obvious to mention'.

Custom and practice

Custom and practice are important sources of implied terms. An employee is presumed to contract with his employer against a background of customs which are 'reasonable , certain, and notorious'.

In *Sagar v Ridehalgh* (1931), deductions from the wages of a cotton-weaver for bad workmanship were upheld by virtue of the existence of a longstanding custom of the trade which was well known.

In *Harwick v Leeds Area Health Authority* (1975), however the applicant was dismissed after exhausting her period of sick pay – which was an entitlement to two months on full pay and two months on half pay. This was in accordance with the normal practice at the time in the Health Service. It was held that such a rule was, in fact, outmoded and unreasonable and that the dismissal was unfair.

Works rules

Employers may issue booklets or post notices containing the rules of the workplace. These may or may not be terms of the contract depending on the circumstances.

Contractual rules

Rules can be express terms:

- if the employee signs an acknowledgment that they are part of the contract;
- if reasonable notice of their existence is given to the employee. The notice must be such that reasonable employees would consider them part of their contract and they must be brought to the notice of employees at or before they enter into the contract.

Rules can also be implied terms in accordance with the above rules, eg the employee has accepted employment on 'the usual conditions'.

Non-contractual rules

Works rules are not necessarily contractual in character.

In *Secretary of State v ASLEF* (1972), Lord Denning stated that the British Railways Rule Book, although signed by each employee, was in no way a contract of employment. They were 'instructions to a man as to how he should do his work'. The distinction is important because the terms of the contract can only be changed by agreement, whereas unilaterally imposed instructions may be changed unilaterally by the employer.

In *Cresswell v Board of Inland Revenue* (1984), employees of the inland revenue refused to cooperate in using computers as they believed that it could lead to a loss of jobs. They claimed a customary right to do the job manually. It was held that the employer could require them to do what was the same job but by different methods.

Variation of contractual terms

The terms of the contract of employment may only be varied with the consent of both parties and there is no power which entitles one side to act unilaterally.

If the employer unilaterally varies the contract and:

- the employee leaves as a result – this will amount to 'constructive dismissal' by the employer; or
- the employee stays on – then

    (a) this may be taken to be an implied acceptance of the changed terms. In *Aparau v Iceland Frozen Foods* (1996), however, the EAT distinguished between contractual terms such as pay rates which have an immediate effect and mobility terms which may not. Care must be taken before deciding that staying on without protest indicates acceptance of mobility terms. In that case an employee claimed constructive dismissal when her employers required her to move to another store in accordance with a mobility clause which they had unilaterally introduced a year previously. It was held that she was constructively dismissed;

    (b) if the employee refuses to agree to the change – there will be a breach of contract on the part of the employer.

    In *Rigby v Ferodo Ltd* (1988), the court accepted that the employees had not agreed to a reduction in their wages by Ferodo and allowed a claim for back pay. Where an employee protests about the change, but stays on it is a question of fact in each case whether he has accepted the change.

However:

- the express terms of the contract may permit a variation;
- a contract may be varied by virtue of a collective agreement;
- a contract of employment cannot remain static permanently. If an employee refuses to accept a variation, there will be no wrongful dismissal provided the correct notice is given. The dismissal may also be fair on the grounds of 'some other substantial reason' provided that the employer can show:

  (a) the change is necessary or desirable from the point of view of the business;

  (b) the employee was fully informed and consulted with regard to the variation;

  (c) due consideration was given to any objections and alternative suggestions; and

  (d) the employer has acted reasonably throughout.

See Chapter 5 – Unfair dismissal.

Overriding terms

Can the implied term of mutual trust and confidence (see below) override an express term of the contract, eg a mobility clause concerning either geographical or task mobility. Does it require the employer to apply the express terms in a reasonable manner?

- If a mobility clause is vague (but not if it is clear according to the EAT) then it must be interpreted in a reasonable manner by the employer (*Rank Xerox v Churchill* (1988)).
- Even where it is explicit, the EAT held in *United Bank v Akhtar* (1989) that the employer must apply the mobility clause in accordance with the implied term of trust and respect. In that case, the court found, despite the presence of a mobility clause, that Akhtar had been constructively dismissed when he was ordered to move from Leeds to Birmingham, on six days' notice.

In *White v Reflecting Roadstuds Ltd* (1991), however, the EAT refused to find constructive dismissal when an employee was transferred to a lower paid job. They distinguished *Akhtar* by stating that that case decided that employers could not enforce an express term in such a way as to prevent the employee from performing his contract. They also suggested that the employer would have to establish reasonable or sufficient grounds for the move.

Implied terms

Terms implied by law (as distinct from terms implied in fact – see 'agreed terms') have been described as legal duties masquerading as contractual terms. Such duties have been imposed by the courts and are implied into every contract of employment.

Duties of the employer

1 To pay the employee

This is the most fundamental duty of the employer. It provides consideration for the contract.

- Suspension without pay on any ground would therefore constitute a breach of contract on the part of the employer, unless such procedure was allowed by an express term of the contract, or was implied by custom or practice. In *Bird v British Celanese* (1945), an employee was suspended for two days in accordance with the firm's practice. This was held to be valid.

- The rate of pay may be expressly agreed between the parties or specified in a collective agreement. In most cases it will be clear as it will have been stated in the 'written particulars' (see above) and in the 'itemised pay statement ' (see below). However, if the statutory statements have not been issued and neither the contract nor a collective agreement says anything, then a 'reasonable' amount must be paid.

- At common law, the general rule is that an employer must pay the wages of all employees if they are available for work, even though none is provided by the employer. However, if the lack of work is due to circumstances beyond the control of the employer then there is no obligation to pay wages, as was the case in *Browning v Crumlin Valley Colleries* (1926), where a mine became unsafe due to flooding and work had to be stopped. It was held that there was no need to pay wages. This general right to be paid may be excluded by express or implied agreement or by custom. Many collective agreements now provide for a 'guaranteed week'. (See also Chapter 3 – Guarantee payments.)

- Details of any provisions relating to sick pay should have been included in the'written particulars'. However, if none have been supplied then, according to *Mears v Safecar Security* (1982), a tribunal must look at all the surrounding circumstances, including whether sick pay had been paid in the past. The presumption in favour of sick pay will only be effective if there was absolutely no other evidence to go on. In *Aspen v Webbs Poultry and Meat Group* (1996), the High Court held that where there was a permanent health insurance scheme which provided for the payment of three-quarters of salary to incapacitated employees until their death, retirement or dismissal, there was an implied term that the express contractual provisions on dismissal would not be used so as to remove the employees' entitlement to the insurance. (See Chapter 3 – Statutory sick pay.)

2 To provide work

The employer does not have a duty to provide work except;

- in the case of piece work or payment by commission;

  In *Turner v Goldsmith* (1891) it was held that a commercial traveller must be allowed a reasonable opportunity to earn his commission which was his sole means of remuneration.

- where it is necessary in order to enable a reputation to be acquired or maintained, eg in acting or journalism;

- where provision of work is necessary in order to maintain an employee's skill or contacts in his profession. In *Provident Financial v Hayward* (1989), the question 'Will the skill atrophy?' was used as a test by the court when dealing with an injunction to prevent an accountant working for a rival firm during 'garden leave'.

3 To provide for the safety of the employees

An employer may be liable:

- directly – for his own breach of duty; or

- indirectly – an employer is vicariously liable for the negligence of his servants during the course of their employment.

An employer has a duty to take reasonable care for the safety of his employees In *Wilson & Clyde Coal Co Ltd v English* (1938), the House of Lords laid down that the employer's duty of care included a duty to provide and maintain:

- safe plant and equipment

  The employer must ensure that the place of work is safe, that he has provided a suitable, sufficient, and safe plant, where it is needed and which is well-maintained. If a plant which has been obtained from a reputable third party is found to be defective then, at common law, the employer would not be liable. However, the Employers Liability (Defective Equipment) Act 1969 provides that the employer shall be liable in those circumstances to the employee and he may then seek reimbursement from the supplier

– safe system and method of work

This is the widest duty and covers such matters as the general conditions of work, coordination of work departments, training and supervision. In *Bux v Slough Metals* (1973), Bux was provided with safety goggles but declined to use them. It was held that the employers had fulfilled their duty to provide suitable equipment, but had failed in the duty to provide adequate training and supervision.

It covers not only physical injuries, but also psychological harm, such as a nervous breakdown caused by stress (*Walker v Northumberland CC* (1995)). It can apply to accidents which occur outside of the employer's premises, as in *General Cleaning Contractors v Christmas* (1953), where a window cleaner fell when cleaning a client's windows. The employers were held responsible for not providing a safe system of work.

– competent staff of fellow employees

This too will cover supervision and training and also horseplay. In *Hudson v Ridge Manufacturing Co Ltd* (1957), Hudson was injured by a practical joke played by a fellow employee who was a notorious practical joker. It was held that the employer was liable.

Alternatively instead of suing his employer for breach of the implied term of the contract, an employee who has been injured at work may sue in the tort of negligence or for breach of statutory duty.

4 To indemnify the employee for expenses properly incurred in the performance of his work.

5 To deal promptly with grievances

In *Goold v McConnel* (1995), salesmen had approached the company on a number of occasions seeking to discuss their grievances concerning a new sales scheme. After the company had failed to respond to several such requests, the salesmen resigned and claimed constructive dismissal. No written statement had been supplied. The EAT held that it is an implied term of the contract of employment that the employer would reasonably and promptly afford an opportunity for its employees to obtain redress of their grievance; a failure to do this would be a fundamental breach of contract.

It has been suggested that this would be particularly useful in sexual or racial harassment cases, where it is alleged that the employer has failed to deal with the employee's complaints.

6 References

Traditionally there was no legal duty to provide a reference or testimonial. However, if a reference is given, care should be taken to see that the reference is accurate. If a reference contains untrue statements then the employer may be liable:

- to the employee for defamation – however, if he can show that the statement was made in pursuance of a social duty (eg to a prospective employer) then, provided he made the statement in good faith, he will be protected by the defence of 'qualified privilege';

- to the employee in the tort of negligent statements;

- to the employee under an implied duty of care in the contract of employment. In *Spring v Guardian Assurance Plc* (1994), the House of Lords held that an employer who provides a reference has a duty to the employee regarding the preparation of the reference and may be liable to him for economic loss suffered as a result of the employer's negligent misstatements. The duty of care could also arise from an implied term in the contract of employment that, if a reference is given, due care and skill must be exercised. The court did not consider that the law of defamation alone gave the employee sufficient protection. The court also suggested that there are circumstances where it is necessary to imply a term into a contract of employment that the employer will provide the employee with a reference at the request of a prospective employer;

- to the recipient – either for the tort of deceit or negligent statements.

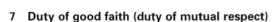

7 Duty of good faith (duty of mutual respect)

This has developed into an important duty in connection with constructive dismissals claims (see Chapter 5). An employer has been held to have broken this duty of good faith when he:

- used abusive language (*Palmanor Ltd v Cedron* (1978));
- made false accusations of theft (*Robinson v Crompton Parkinson* (1978));
- criticised managers in front of subordinates (*Associated Tyre Specialists v Waterhouse* (1976));
- failed to protect an employee against harassment (*Bracebridge Engineering v Darby* (1990)).

Controversy has arisen as to whether this implied duty can be used to limit an employer's exercise of his express powers under the contract. See 'Overriding terms', above.

Duties of the employee

1 To render personal service

The employee must carry out his work personally. He may not delegate his duties.

2 To take care

The employee must carry out his work with proper care and skill.

In *Lister v Romford Ice and Cold Storage Company* (1957), it was held that an employee who injured a fellow employee by his negligent reversing of a vehicle had broken a term of his contract, and would have to reimburse his employer for any losses caused to him. The British Insurance Association has agreed not to insist upon enforcement of this duty in the absence of fraud. The nationalised industries and local authorities follow a similar policy.

3 To obey all reasonable and lawful orders

- The order must be within the terms of employment: in *O'Brien v Associated Fire Alarms* (1968), it was held that an electrician who had been lawfully employed to install fire alarms in Liverpool could lawfully refuse to work in Bradford, 120 miles away.
- It should not require the employee to do something dangerous (*Ottoman Bank v Chakanian* (1930)); or something illegal (*Morrish v Henlys Ltd* (1973)).

- Modern cases tend to take the view that a single and isolated act of disobedience does not amount to an intention to repudiate the whole contract.

Davies and Friedland have pointed out that: 'This implied term has the effect of lodging management prerogative firmly in the centre of the contract of employment.'

4 To give faithful service – 'the duty of fidelity'

'The practical duty in any given case is to find exactly how far the rather vague duty of fidelity extends' *per* Lord Greene MR.

It would seem to cover the following:

- Not to wilfully disrupt the employer's business

    In *Secretary of State v ASLEF* (1972), railwaymen in a 'work to rule' had by a meticulous observance of the rule book brought the railways to a standstill. The Court of Appeal held that they had wilfully embarked on an action which would obstruct the employer's business and bring it to a standstill. To do so would be to break an implied term in their contracts. In *Ticehurst v BT Plc* (1992), Mrs Ticehurst, who was a BT manager and a union official, refused to sign an agreement to work normally and not to withdraw goodwill during a dispute between BT and the union. The Court of Appeal held that her threat to withdraw goodwill amounted to a breach of the implied term that she would serve her employer faithfully. It was necessary to imply this term into a manager's contract because they are in charge of other employees and must exercise judgment and discretion when they give orders.

- Cooperation and adaptability

    In *Sim v Rotherham BC* (1986), a refusal by a teacher to cover for an absent colleague was held to be a breach of the duty to cooperate. In *Cresswell v Board of Inland Revenue* (1984), it was held that the employee's refusal to computerise was a breach of this duty.

- Not to compete

    (a) Spare-time work

        What a worker does in his spare time is normally his own business; however, it has been stated that 'it would be deplorable if it were laid down what a worker could, consistent with his duty to his employer, knowingly, deliberately and secretly set himself to do in his spare time, something which would inflict great harm on his employer's business'. In *Hivac v Park Royal Instruments Ltd* (1946), an injunction was granted against a competitor restraining him from employing the plaintiff's employees from making valves for him in their spare time. It was not necessary to show that any confidential information had been divulged.

(b) Ex-employees

An ex-employee is free to go into competition with his ex-employer. But whilst employed he must not break his duty of fidelity, eg a milk-roundsman may not canvass his customers on his last day at work (*Wessex Dairies v Smith*); a tradesman may not copy out a list of his employer's clients before leaving (*Robb v Green*). However, there was no breach of duty when two junior employees wrote to a supplier for information.

The contract may contain an express restrictive covenant governing an ex-employees conduct.

• Not to divulge any confidential information

The employee must not disclose any confidential information about the employer's business to an unauthorised person. Such information may be as to its profitability, new designs or models or mode of operation or anything relating to the business. This obligation may continue even after the employment has ended. An employee instructed in a secret manufacturing process will be prevented by an injunction from disclosing that process to a rival company whom he later worked for. This rule will not apply if the employee is obliged by law to disclose information under the Health and Safety at Work Act 1974.

The nature of confidential information was explained in *Faccenda Chicken Ltd v Fowler* (1986). Fowler had been employed as Sales Manager of Faccenda Chicken until he resigned along with eight other employees in order to set up a rival business selling fresh chickens from refrigerated vehicles. Neither Fowler nor the other employees were subject to any restrictive covenants. Faccenda claimed that Fowler and the others had broken their contracts by using confidential sales information relating to the requirements of customers and the prices they paid to the detriment of the company. The Court of Appeal laid down the following guidelines with regard to confidential information. Information is confidential if:

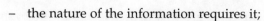

- the nature of the information requires it;
- the nature of the employment requires it;
- the employer has impressed on the employees the confidential nature of the information;
- the confidential information can be isolated from other information which the employee is able to disclose.

Applying these principles, the court held that Fowler and his colleagues had not broken their duty of fidelity – the information they had used was not confidential.

- Whistle-blowing

  There is an exception to the general duty that confidential information must not be disclosed, where the disclosure is in the public interest.

  In *Initial Services v Putterill* (1968), a former employee revealed to the *Daily Mail* that the company was involved with others in a price fixing agreement contrary to the Restrictive Practices Act; and in *Lion Laboratories v Evans* (1985), an ex-employee publicised the fact that the accuracy of a breathalyser used by the police was in doubt. In both cases injunctions against the ex-employees were refused on the ground that the information was in the public interest.

  Normally, in order to be protected by the 'public interest' defence, the information must be accurate. However, in *Re a Company's Application* (1989) where an employee complained to Fimbra, and to the inland revenue, it was held that the fact that both had a duty to investigate such matters meant that the employee did not have to prove the accuracy of his allegations.

- Not to make a secret profit

  For example, taking a secret commission from a supplier, see *Boston Deep Sea Fishing v Ansell* (1888).

Incorporation of terms

Collective agreements between trade unions and employers or employers associations are not legally enforceable. The terms of a collective agreement may however, become enforceable between an individual employer and an individual employee by being incorporated in the employee's contract of employment. It was held in *Marley v Forward Trust* (1986) that a clause in the collective bargain stating 'this is not an enforceable agreement' (TINLEA) does not affect the issue of incorporation.

The following conditions must be satisfied:

1   There must be evidence of an intention to incorporate

There have been suggestions that collective terms should be incorporated into a contract on the basis that the union is negotiating as agent for its members. This has not been pursued as it involves many difficulties, eg the position of later enrolled employees. However, in *Sing v BSC* (1974), it was held that Sing, who had resigned from the union, was not bound by a new shift system which the union had negotiated after his resignation and which he did not wish to observe.

By express incorporation

For example, by a statement in the written terms that the contract is to be subject to the terms of a particular collective bargain.

In *Robertson v British Gas* (1983), the statement read 'The provisions of the Agreement of the Joint National Council will apply to you' and added 'incentive bonus scheme conditions will apply to meter reading and collective work'. It was held that this incorporated the bonus scheme into the employee's contract of employment and, furthermore, the Gas Board could not unilaterally withdraw the scheme as it had become part of the employee's contract of employment. He was entitled to his bonus.

On the other hand if the statement states that the employee is to be bound by the collective agreement in force *for the time being* then the contractual terms can be varied without any further consent on the employee's part. Since the collective agreement itself is not legally binding, the employer can also de-recognise the union and move to individual bargaining without the consent of the employee.

In *Cadoux v Central Regional Council* (1986), rules drawn up by the employer were expressly incorporated into the contract of employment; yet because, as employer's rules, they were subject to unilateral change, it was held that benefits under the rules (which related to a pension scheme) could be removed by the employer's unilateral act.

The contract of employment may be undertaken on the basis of 'union rates of pay' (wages clauses only are incorporated) or 'union conditions' (all the provisions of the collective agreement are incorporated). Employees who work for public institutions are normally engaged on the basis of the appropriate scale laid down by the negotiating bodies, and the only scope for individual bargaining may be on the precise point of entry into the scale.

Implied incorporation

It is also possible to incorporate the terms of a collective agreement into a contract of employment by implication. The most common basis for this is that both employer and employee have consistently behaved as if the agreement was part of the contract, ie incorporation as a result of custom and practice. Professor Khan-Freund has called it 'crystallised custom'. It was held, however, in *Hamilton v Futura Floors* (1991), that an employer's membership of a trade association will not alone be enough to incorporate a term into an employee's contract.

2   The term must be suitable for incorporation

Some terms of the collective bargain are unsuitable for incorporation as they are intended to govern managerial relations rather than the rights of individual employees, eg conciliation procedures, union recognition rights or redundancy procedures.

In *British Leyland v McQuilken* (1978), the collective agreement provided that on the closure of a department, employees would have a choice between retraining and redundancy. After a change in management policy, McQuillen was offered a choice between transfer to another location or redundancy. The EAT overturned the tribunal's finding of constructive dismissal, stating that 'the collective provision was a long-term plan dealing with policy rather than the rights of individual employees'. In *Young v Canadian Northern Railway Co* (1931), the Privy Council held that a redundancy scheme providing for 'Last In First Out' (LIFO) was not incorporated. In *Marley v Forward Trust* (1986), however, the Court of Appeal held that collective agreement providing for a six-month trial in a new job or a redundancy could be relied on by the employee.

In *Alexander v Standard Telephones & Cables* (1991), the EAT held that a selection process, LIFO, was not suitable for incorporation, but enhanced rights of pay for redeployed workers were incorporated; in that case, wages were specifically referred to in the written terms.

Duty to inform

It was held in *Scally v Southern Health and Social Services Board* (1991), that, where there are changes to the incorporated collective agreement to the employee's advantage, the employer has a duty to so inform the employee. In that case, the plaintiffs who were doctors in Northern Ireland sued their employers for the failure to inform them of a new right to purchase added years of pension entitlement.

Query

Does this also imply a duty to inform employees of changes to their disadvantage?

'No strike' clauses

Considerable difficulties have been experienced in the past with 'no strike' clauses. A great deal may depend on the precise wording, eg 'the union will not call a strike until the procedure for settling the dispute is exhausted'. This is an obligation on the union and is unsuitable for incorporation However, 'the employees will not go on strike until procedures for settling the dispute is exhausted' is capable of incorporation.

Section 180 of the TULR(C)A 1992 now provides that such a clause will not be binding unless:

- the collective agreement is in writing;
- it expressly states that the term is to be incorporated into the individual contract;
- a copy of the collective agreement is reasonably accessible to the employees concerned;
- the individual contract expressly or impliedly incorporates such a term.

3 Statutory rights for employees during the course of employment

You should be familiar with the following areas:

- the concept of 'continuity of employment'
- the effect of the Transfer of Undertakings Regulations
- statutory provisions on pay
- restrictions on deductions from pay
- maternity rights
- 'time off' entitlements
- 'working time' legislation, including directives awaiting implementation

Most rights for employees both during and on termination of employment are now found in the Employment Rights Act (ERA) 1996, but there are still some matters which are included in other legislation, eg The Transfer of Undertakings Regulations (TUPE) 1981, The Social Security Contributions and Benefits Act 1992, and the Trade Union and Labour Relations (Consolidation) Act (TULR(C)A) 1993.

Many of the rights are free-standing, eg time off entitlements, but others, such as the requirements for 'continuous employment' and the meaning of a 'weeks pay' are to be read in conjunction with other rights such as unfair dismissal, redundancy payments (see Chapters 5, 6, 7 and 8) or guarantee payment (see below).

Continuity of employment

Most rights granted by the ERA 1996 whether during employment, or on its termination, are dependent on the employee having a certain period of 'continuous employment'. It is important in ascertaining who is qualified for those rights and also in some cases in computing what benefits are due, eg in the case of redundancy payments.

Prior to 1994, 'continuous employment' could only be claimed by employees who worked for at least 16 hours a week or eight hours a week if they had worked for that employer for five years.

In March 1994, however, the House of Lords declared in *R v Secretary of State for Employment, ex p EOC* that the minimum hours thresholds were incompatible with community law, and the ERA 1996 does not now require any minimum hours worked per week in order to qualify for continuous employment.

Retrospective claims

In *Biggs v Somerset CC* (1995) and *McManus v Display Foods Ltd* (1995), the Employment Appeal Tribunal (EAT) considered what national time limits were applicable to claims from part-timers dismissed in the 1970s. The EAT declared that the time limits contained in the EP(C)A 1978 applied, ie three months for unfair dismissal and six months for redundancy payments. The court stated that the Treaty of Rome did not confer a right to unfair dismissal or redundancy payments, it simply operated to remove the offending conditions which were considered discriminatory. As the claims were brought under the EP(C)A 1978, the time limited in that Act applied.

The most controversial aspects of the rulings centred on the question of when time began to run. The employees argued, that as their claims were based on the direct effect of Article 119, the relevant time limits did not begin to run until it became clear that the hours thresholds in the EP(C)A 1978 contravened Article 119.

The basis of EAT's decision in both cases was that the employees could have relied on the direct effect of Article 119 at the time of their dismissal to challenge the discriminatory hours thresholds then in operation. The Court of Appeal upheld the ruling.

Weeks which count (s 212 of the ERA 1996)

Continuity begins on the day the employee starts work under the contract. If, however, the starting day is a non-working day, eg a bank holiday then continuity will start on that day although he does not actually start work until the following day (*Salvation Army v Dewsbury* (1984)).

The following weeks count towards continuous employment:

- Weeks covered by a contract of employment – providing the contract of employment subsists there is continuity even if the employee does not actually work, eg because of absence due to holiday, sickness, injury, pregnancy or confinement.

- Weeks not covered by a contract of employment – even where there is no subsisting contract of employment there is continuity in the following four circumstances:

(i) Where an employee is absent through sickness or injury for up to 26 weeks. However, if an employee is away through illness and then remains away for pension purposes there will not be continuity (*Pearson v Kent CC* (1992)).

(ii) Where an employee is absent from work on account of a temporary cessation of work, eg lack of orders, fire, strike at a suppliers. The cessation must refer to the employees work; the employer may still be carrying on business. The temporary nature of the cessation will be judged on the basis of hind sight.

In *Bentley Engineering v Crown* (1976), two years absence on account of redundancy was held to be a 'temporary absence'.

In *Ford v Warwickshire CC* (1983), the phrase was held to cover the case of a school teacher who had been employed on eight consecutive fixed term contracts for the academic year (September to July). The summer vacations were held not to break continuity. It did not matter that the cessations were predictable and regular.

(iii) Where an employee is absent and by arrangement or custom the employment is considered as continuing, eg secondment or leave of absence for personal reasons.

In *Wishart v National Coal Board* (1974), an employee of the National Coal Board did not lose continuity when he worked for a year for a firm which carried out development work for the Coal Board.

In *Lloyds Bank v Secretary of State for Employment* (1979), it was held that a bank employee who worked one week on, one week off was absent 'by arrangement'.

(iv) Where an employee is absent from work because of *pregnancy* or *confinement* up to a limit of 26 weeks.

But if the employee returns to work in accordance with the statutory maternity leave provisions: then all the weeks in which she was away will count.

Note

- Employment is presumed to be continuous unless the contrary is shown.

- Continuity means employment with a certain employer; it is not broken because the employee has been moved to a new department, or has been promoted.

- An employee who is re-engaged or reinstated as a result of a tribunal order or ACAS conciliation or a private agreement will not have suffered a break in employment. The weeks away will also count towards his years of employment.

- Certain weeks when the employee is on strike, or is working abroad, *do not count towards continuity of employment, but do not break continuity.*

Change of employer (s 218 of the ERA 1996)

Continuity is preserved in some cases even where there is a change of employer. Where the respective employers agree to this the 'written particulars' should record this fact.

- Where the trade or business is transferred:

    There must be a transfer of the business not merely a transfer of the assets. In *Melon v Hector Powe* (1981) a factory which manufactured 'made to measure' men's suits was bought by a firm who used the premises to manufacture 'ready made' suits but only after they had completed the work in progress. Held by the Court of Appeal: there was no transfer of the business.

    There must be a transfer of goodwill not merely a business opportunity (*Bumstead v John Carr Ltd* (1967)).

    The employee must be employed at the 'moment of transfer' (*Teeside Times v Drury* (1980)).

    The burden of proving the transfer is on the employee:

    o where an Act of Parliament causes one company to replace another;

    o where the employer is a partnership, personal representatives or a trust and the composition is changed;

    o where the employee is employed by an associated company, ie a company of which the other has control, directly or indirectly, or if both companies are controlled by a third person;

o   where the employee is employed by a school maintained by a LEA and is transferred to another school or LEA;

o   where there is a relevant transfer under The Transfer of Undertakings Regulations 1981 (see TUPE).

Transfer of Undertakings Regulations (TUPE) 1981 – as amended by TURERA 1993

It is important to note that where the ownership of a business is changed through a transfer of shares, eg in a takeover bid, there is no change of employer. The employees are still employed by the same corporate entity, ie the company and none of the following provisions apply. Where a business is transferred from one person to another person, the following rules may apply.

At common law
Contracts of employment are not transferred.

See *Nokes v Doncaster Amalgamated Colliery* (1940). The transfer of the business is treated as a fundamental breach of contract which allows the employee to leave and claim breach of contract.

Under s 218 of the Employment Rights Act 1996 – see above

Under TUPE 1981
These were introduced in order to comply with the Acquired Rights Directive, and must be interpreted in accordance with the directive.

They provide for the automatic transfer of:

*   contracts of employment – ie all rights, powers, duties and liabilities under or in connection with such contract, except any provision relating to occupational pension schemes;
*   collective agreements;
*   trade union recognition;

to the transferee, in the case of a relevant transfer.

They also make it automatically unfair to dismiss an employee for any reason connected with the transfer unless it is for an economic, technical, or organisational reason connected with a change in the workforce.

The regulations and the directive were introduced in order to protect the rights of employees and cannot be used to transfer a contract of employment against the employees will. In *Katsikas v Konstantinidis* (1993) it was held by the European Court of Justice (ECJ) that an employee can resist an automatic transfer of his contract.

The regulations now provide that an employee may terminate a contract of employment if he objects to being transferred to the transferee, but this is not to operate as a dismissal, so that there is no entitlement to unfair dismissal compensation or redundancy payments.

The initial legislation was introduced unenthusiastically by the government and had to be amended in TURERA 1993 after the European Commission had commenced infringement proceedings.

Problem areas in the regulations

1 What is a 'relevant transfer'?

Originally, the definition excluded any undertaking which was not in the 'nature of a commercial venture'. This, however, was changed in TURERA 1993 following the decision of the ECJ in *Dr Sophie Redmond Stitchung v Bartol* (1992) where it was held that a transfer of a subsidy from a local authority from one foundation dedicated to helping drug addicts to another was capable of constituting a transfer under the directive.

The government, however, still argued that there had to be a transfer of an 'undertaking' or 'business' not merely the transfer of a 'function' or 'activity'.

This argument, also, was defeated in *Rask v ISS* (1993) where the ECJ held the directive covered the situation where Philips had contracted out its canteen services to ISS, who would receive a fee from which labour, management and administrative costs would be met. Philips would provide the premises, equipment, refuse collection and cleaning products. ISS would offer employment to Philips employees.

It was again defeated in *Christel Schmidt*, etc (1994) where it was held that the directive covered a situation where a bank transferred to a cleaning company the cleaning of a branch which had previously been cleaned by one employee.

Note

A Draft Revised Directive has now been issued which draws a distinction between the transfer of 'an undertaking or business' and the 'transfer of an activity'.

2 What is a 'transfer'?

Originally the courts in this country exclude from a 'transfer' a change in the holder of a franchise or the emergence of a new contractor when a fixed term contract had ended, on the ground that there was no direct transfer. But following certain decisions of the ECJ that view has been changed.

In *Daddy's Dance Hall* (1988) it was held that the directive covered the termination of a non-transferable lease over a restaurant and bar and the granting of a new lease.

In *P Bork A/S* (1989) it was held that the forfeiture of a lease over a factory followed by the sale of the freehold to a new owner could amount to a 'transfer'.

In *Dines v Initial Health Care Services* (1994), the Court of Appeal ruled that the regulations did apply to a second phase contracting out where a cleaning contract which had originally been awarded to Initial Health Care Services under a competitive tendering process was granted to a new company on the expiration of the first contract. It confirmed that the transfer could take place in two stages – first, by handing back the cleaning to the authority and then the authority granting the contract to a new firm. The decisive criterion seems to be whether there has been a transfer of an 'economic entity' which retains its identity after the change has taken place'.

The EAT held in *Farmer v Danzas* (1993) that the crucial time in which an economic entity has been retained is immediately after the transfer. The fact that the transferee later integrated the work with his own business did not alter the position.

In *Ryegaard* (1995), the ECJ introduced a further criterion. In addition to the undertaking retaining its identity it had to be stable and capable of continuation. In that case, a company sub-contracted a specific task to another company, which in turn assigned some of the work to another company.

Note

However, a shift of emphasis is seen in *Suzen v Zehnacker Gebausereinigung ets* (1997), where the ECJ, whilst confirming that a relevant transfer required an identifiable economic entity that had retained its identity after the transfer, ruled that the directive does not necessarily apply when a contracted out service is transferred from one contractor to another. The directive only applies if the change of contractor involves *the transfer of significant tangible or intangible assets or the major part of the workforce who provided the service prior to the change in contractor*. They also pointed out that an entity cannot be reduced merely to the activity entrusted to it.

The ruling was followed by the Court of Appeal in *Betts & Ors v Brintel Helicopters* (1997), where it was held that TUPE did not apply to a change in the contractors providing contracted-out helicopter services to a third party as there was no transfer of assets or employees. The decision applied to a second generation contracting out, but the court expressed the opinion that there is no logical distinction between first generation contracting-out, and a subsequent change of contractors.

3   Was the employee employed immediately before the transfer?

In *Secretary of State for Employment v Spence* (1987), it was held that only employees employed at the very moment of the business transfer had their contracts transferred to the buyer. An employee dismissed by the vendor of the business four hours before the transfer was not covered by the regulations.

However, in *Litster v Forth Dry Dock & Engineering* (1990) the House of Lords confirmed *Spence* but held that an employee dismissed by the vendor 'for a reason connected with the transfer was covered'. In order to comply with the directive the regulations must be read to include 'or would have been so employed if he had not been unfairly dismissed for a reason connected with the transfer'. So an employee dismissed at the behest of the transferee will be dismissed in connection with the transfer.

In *Ibex Trading v Walton* (1994), the Employment Appeal Tribunal (EAT) confirmed that every dismissal aimed at making a business more attractive to a buyer would not fall within TUPE. If no offer had yet been made, no collusion had taken place, then the dismissal is not in connection with the transfer. (The transferee was insolvent in that case.)

In *Longden v Ferrari* (1994) EAT held:

(a) where there is a series of transactions leading to a sale, the transfer takes place on the actual sale;

(b) a transfer is not to be considered a principal reason for a dismissal where the prospective purchaser selects whom he wishes to retain, but places no pressure on the transferor to dismiss. (A conclusion much criticised.)

Statutory provisions on pay

The employees right to remuneration is governed like the other terms of the contract of employment, by:

• agreement;

- collective agreements;
- terms implied by the common law;
- terms imposed by legislation.

These legislative provisions must be read in conjunction with the implied duties of an employer to pay his employees (see Chapter 2).

Amount of remuneration

At present there are no requirements for minimum wages to be paid; the Wages Councils which provided for minimum rates of pay in certain industries were abolished in 1986. The Labour government is proposing to introduce legislation on a minimum wage but this awaits the recommendation of a committee set up to consider the rate at which it should be set.

The rate of remuneration may be expressly agreed between the parties or specified in a collective agreement.

In most cases it will be clear, as it will have been:

- stated in the 'written particulars' required by ss 1–7 of the ERA 1996 (see Chapter 2).
- stated in the 'itemised pay statement' required by ss 6–8 of the ERA 1996.

However, if the statutory statements have not been issued and neither a contract nor a collective agreement says anything specific, the employee can claim to be paid a reasonable amount on a *quantum meruit* basis.

'Weeks pay' ss 221–24 of the ERA 1996

The phrase 'weeks pay' is used in relation to certain benefits, eg redundancy payments or compensation for unfair dismissal. It is to be calculated as follows:

- Where there are normal hours of work, and the remuneration does not vary, then 'weeks pay' is the amount paid under the contract of employment.

  It was held in *Tarmac Roadstone Holdings Ltd v Peacock* (1973) that for overtime to be included it must be obligatory on both employer and employee. It will, however, include contractually binding commission and bonus payments.

- Where there are normal working hours, but the remuneration varies with the amount of work done, eg in respect of piece work, then the weeks pay is the pay for the normal working hours at the average hourly rate. The average hourly rate is calculated by dividing the total amount of pay received during the last 12 working weeks (minus overtime pay as above) by the number of hours worked during that time.

• If there are no normal hours, then the weekly pay is calculated by establishing the average weekly pay over the preceding working weeks.

Note
If for some reason the employee is not at work one week that would not feature as part of the 'working weeks'. However, if his remuneration has been reduced as a result of a shortage of work during the last 12 weeks, that would affect his average weekly pay.

Sick pay

Contractual
Under ERA 1996 details of any terms relating to sick pay should be given in the written particulars. The position should therefore be clear. However, if no written particulars are supplied or their accuracy is challenged, then the court may have to consider the possibility of an implied term (see Chapter 2).

Statutory sick pay
Employees are entitled under the Social Security Contributions and Benefits Act 1992 to statutory sick pay (SSP) for the first 28 weeks of sickness. There is a legal obligation on all employees to pay SSP with no contracting-out by agreement with employees.

The scheme was originally introduced in order to transfer the ad ministration of the old sickness benefit scheme to the employer. Since 1994, however, only employers employing less than 20 employees may recover the money from the government.

Main provisions
The employee must be suffering from some disease or physical or mental disability which renders him incapable of work, and

• the period of incapacity must be a period of four or more consecutive days (which may include Sundays or holidays).

Two periods of incapacity are treated as one if they are not separated by more than two weeks.

- The period of incapacity will start with the incapacity for work and end with the first of the following:

(i) the day the employee returns to work;

(ii) after 28 days;

(iii) the termination of the contract; or

(iv) a pregnant employee reaches the beginning of the 11th week before the expected week of confinement.

The method by which the employee is to notify his employer is a matter for agreement between them.

Pay during lay-offs or short-time working

For position at common law, see Chapter 2. Due to the rather uncertain position at common law, collective agreements now cover a wide range of employees. These often have the effect of guaranteeing workers some of their wages during the first few days, weeks or months of the lay-off.

A statutory right to payment in the event of lay-offs is provided in ss 28–34 of the ERA 1996. This provides that where employees are laid off because:

(a) there is a diminution in the requirements of the employers business; or

(b) any other event which affects the employers business,

there must be made a guarantee payment of up to a maximum daily rate specified from time to time for up to five days in any three-month period. There is no right to a guarantee payment, however, if the lay-offs are due to a trade dispute involving any employee of the employer or of an associated employer.

To be eligible the employee must:

- have at least one month's continuous service;

- be laid off for the whole of his normal working hours;

- not have unreasonably refused an offer of alternative employment;

- be available for work.

Employers who have entered into a collective agreement may be exempted from the statutory requirements.

Where an employer fails to make a guarantee payment, an industrial tribunal can order him to do so.

Suspension on medical grounds (ss 64–65 of the ERA 1996)

An employee with one month's continuous employment is entitled to up to six months' pay if he is suspended from work in accordance with legislation made under the Health and Safety at Work Act 1974, eg Control of Lead at Work Regulations; Ionising Radiation Regulations; Control of Substances Hazardous to Health Regulations.

He is not entitled to payment under this section, however, if:

• he is not fit for work.

  In *Satellite Batteries Ltd v Appleton*, the employee was certified unfit for work by his doctor after falling into a skip containing lead paste. Held: he was not entitled to a payment for suspension.

• he turns down suitable alternative employment; or

• he does not make himself available for work.

Suspension on maternity grounds

An employer must suspend from work:

• a woman of child-bearing age doing work which could involve a risk to the health or safety of a new or expectant mother or her baby;

• a new or expectant mother working at night who has a medical certificate advising her not to work at night.

A woman who is suspended on maternity grounds is entitled to her full pay for all the time she is suspended, unless she has turned down an offer of suitable alternative work. No period of continuous employment is required.

Protection against deductions (ss 13–27, Part 11 of the ERA 1996)

These are now found in the ERA 1996, but were originally introduced in the Wages Act 1986 which stated as its purpose: 'To replace ancient and obsolete laws by a comprehensive, easily understood, easily enforceable and fairer set of statutory rights for all workers, manual and non-manual.'

The Wages Act 1986 repealed the Truck Acts which applied to manual workers and which required them to be paid in 'coin of the realm'. Workers may, therefore, now be paid by cheque or credit transfer.

The Truck Acts also controlled deductions from manual workers pay, requiring them to be fair and reasonable. The ERA controls deductions from the wages of all employees, but does not require the deductions to be 'fair and reasonable'.

Section 13 makes any deduction unlawful unless it is authorised in one of the following ways:

- by statute – eg PAYE;

- by a term in the contract – provided the contract is in writing, or the term is notified in writing to the employee before the deduction is made.

  It was held in *York City Travel v Smith* (1990) that provided the consent or agreement is given before the event (in this case a collective agreement) and the written notice is given before the deduction is made the deduction will be valid. However, written notice must be given to each worker individually. In *Kerr v Sweater Shop* (1996) it was held that a notice displayed on · a notice board was not sufficient.

- by the specific consent of the employee, signified in writing – the agreement must predate the event which gave rise to the deduction. In *Discount Tobacco & Confectionery Ltd v Williamson* (1993) large stock deficiencies were discovered by the employer in February. In March, the manager signed an agreement allowing the employer to deduct £3500 from his wages at the rate of £20 a week. The employer quoted s 1(4) which states that any agreement by the worker shall not operate to authorise a deduction made before the agreement was signed and argued that the agreement had to predate only the deduction. The EAT disagreed, the agreement had to predate the event giving rise to the deduction. The deductions prior to the agreement in March were therefore in valid.

Wages are defined (s 27) as any sum payable to the worker by the employer in connection with the employment, including 'any fee, bonus, commission, holiday pay, or other emolument referable to his employment, whether payable under the contract or otherwise'.

In *Delaney v Staples* (1992), the applicant had been summarily dismissed, but was given a cheque for £82 as payment in lieu of notice. The cheque was later stopped. The applicant also claimed to be entitled to a commission and holiday pay amounting to £55. The House of Lords held that 'payments in lieu' were not wages, but were damages for breach of contract.

In *Kent Management Services Ltd v Butterfield* (1992), it was held that commission and bonus schemes which were stated to be *ex gratia* and not payable in exceptional circumstances were 'wages' within the meaning of the Act when they had been calculated and where there were no exceptional circumstances. But in *London Borough of Southwark v O'Brian* (1996) the EAT held that withdrawing car expenses did not breach the above provisions as these were 'expenses' not 'wages'.

Section 13(3) provides that 'Where the total amount of any wages paid on any occasion ... is less than the total amount of wages that are *properly payable* to him, then except in so far as the deficiency is attributable to an error in computation, the amount of the deficiency shall be treated ... as a *deduction*.' It is for the tribunal to decide what sums are 'properly payable' using the principles of the law of contract (*Yemm v British Steel* (1994)).

It was confirmed in *Delaney v Staples* that total non-payment can qualify as a deduction, and in *Bruce v Wiggins Teape* (1994), where the employer unilaterally withdrew an enhanced contractually agreed overtime and the employees continued to work under protest, the EAT held there was no distinction between a *reduction* and a *deduction*.

In *Morgan v West Glamorgan CC* (1995), the EAT again confirmed that a decision to demote an employee and reduce his salary resulting from an erroneous view of the legal and factual position was a deduction. It also held that an erroneous view of the legal and factual position was not a computation error.

Section 14 contains a list of exceptions to which s 1 does not apply:

- overpayment of wages or expenses.
- disciplinary proceedings held by virtue of statutory provisions. This has been held to refer only to some public employments. Disciplinary proceedings recommended by ACAS will not qualify (*Chiltern House v Chambers* (1990)).
- A statutory requirement to deduct wages to pay over to a public authority.
- Payments agreed by the employee which are made over to a third party.
- A strike or other industrial action in which the employee took part.
- The satisfaction of a court or a tribunal order requiring the employee to pay something to the employer.

These deductions will not infringe the Act if they are otherwise lawful, ie there is power to make these deductions under the common law. However, in *Sunderland Polytechnic v Evans* (1993), it was held that the tribunal could not investigate whether there was a right to deduct money as a result of industrial action by the employee – this was a common law matter for the civil courts to examine. The employer need only state that the deduction fell within one of these exceptions. The same decision was reached in *SIP (Industrial Products) v Swinn* (1994), where an employer deducted a sum of money from wages to cover money which the employee had dishonestly obtained. The EAT said it was not for the tribunal to decide on the lawfulness of a deduction under s 14. This was a matter for the civil courts.

The confusion concerning jurisdiction and the need to go to the county court will be less since the Industrial Tribunals Extension of Jurisdiction Order 1994 which provides that an employee may bring a claim for up to £25,000 before an industrial tribunal for breach of contract or for a sum due under that contract if the claim arises or is outstanding on the termination of employment. However, jurisdiction will still remain an issue where there is no termination as in *Sunderland Polytechnic v Evans*.

There are similar provisions to the above governing payment by an employee to his employer.

Retail workers (ss 17–22 of the ERA 1996)

This relates to workers involved in the supply of goods or services.

Retail contracts often contain onerous terms requiring workers to make good cash shortages or stock deficiencies. Section 13 (above) applies to retail workers and s 17 provides that the deduction must not exceed 10% of the gross wage on any one occasion. This does not apply, however, to the final payment when there is no limit.

Deductions must be made within 12 months.

Complaints to an industrial tribunal (s 23)

A worker may make a complaint to an industrial tribunal within three months of the deduction.

Note
It is now automatically unfair to dismiss an employee for exercising a statutory right. See Chapter 7.

Maternity rights

Four basic rights exist in connection with pregnancy:
- a right to time off for ante-natal care;
- a right not to be dismissed on the grounds of pregnancy;

- a right to maternity pay; and
- a right to maternity leave.

Time off for ante-natal care

A woman has a right to paid time off in order to attend an ante-natal appointment advised by a doctor, midwife or health visitor. The employer is entitled to ask for proof of the appointment and of the pregnancy. If the employer unreasonably refuses her request, then she may complain to an industrial tribunal, which may award a sum equal to the sum she should have been paid for time off.

Dismissal on the ground of pregnancy (s 99 of the ERA 1996)

A dismissal on the ground of pregnancy is automatically unfair (see Chapter 7).

Maternity pay (Part XII Social Security and Benefits Act 1992)

There are three rates of maternity pay or maternity allowances. These are separate from any contractual entitlement which the employee may have.

(i) Statutory maternity pay

A woman who:

- has had 26 weeks' continuous employment at the 15th week before the expected date of confinement; and
- whose average earnings are at, or above, the lower limit for paying national insurance contributions is entitled to 18 weeks' maternity pay from her employer.

This consists of:
- six weeks' pay at 90% of her salary; and
- 12 weeks at the higher rate of statutory sick pay.

A woman so qualified can choose when she wants her maternity pay to start.

(ii) Maternity allowance

A woman who:

- has worked and made national insurance contributions for 26 out of the last 66 weeks before the expected date of birth; and

- is employed on the 15th week before the expected date of birth is entitled to a maternity allowance which is equal to the statutory sick pay at the higher rate.

(iii) Maternity allowance

A woman who:

- has worked for 26 weeks out of the last 66 weeks; but
- is not employed at the 15th week before the expected date of birth is entitled to a lower rate maternity allowance which is equal to the statutory sick pay at the lower rate.

In all cases, the pregnant woman must give her employer 21 days' notice in writing of her intended absence. The employer may set off 92% of the 12-week element against national insurance contributions, unless a small employer (paying less than £20,000 per annum in National Insurance contributions) who can set off 105.5%.

Maternity leave (ss 71–85 of the ERA 1996)

(i) Maternity leave

All women are entitled to a minimum of 14 weeks' maternity leave regardless of their length of service or hours per week worked. It may commence any time after the 11th week before the expected date of birth on any day designated by the woman.

A woman who needs to be away on medical grounds before the 11th week may claim statutory sick pay. If she is away sick at any time within six weeks of the expected date of birth, then the start of her maternity leave is triggered automatically.

During maternity leave, she is entitled to all benefits under her contract except pay.

(ii) Maternity absence

A woman who has been continually employed for two years at the 11th week before the expected birth may claim her right to return to work any time before the end of the 29th week after the date of her actual confinement.

Note

- Her contract should still be in operation on the 11th week – she does not actually need to have been at work.
- She may commence her leave any time after the 11th week – which allows her a total of 40 weeks.

- There are very complicated notice requirements which the pregnant woman must comply with in order to qualify for the above provisions.

Notice requirements for both maternity leave and maternity absence.

(1) Twenty-one days at least before her leave is due to start, she must give notice in writing to the employer that she is pregnant, and also the expected day of her confinement.

(2) She must give 15 days' notice of when her leave will start, this may be combined with the above.

(3) If leave commences early because of absence within six weeks of the expected date of confinement or because of early birth, she must serve notice of this to the employer as soon as possible – in writing if so requested by the employer.

(4) The employer may require, in writing, not less than 10 days before the end of the 14/29 week period, whether she still intends to exercise her right to return. He must also specify what would happen if she fails to respond. To preserve her right to return, she must respond positively within 14 days.

(5) Finally, she must give at least 21 days' notice of her intention to return.

(6) If she wishes to return before the end of her 14-day notice, she must give her employer seven days' notice of this.

(7) A woman entitled to up to 40 weeks' maternity leave may, in certain circumstances, delay her return for a period of up to four weeks provided she supplies a medical certificate. It was held by the EAT in *Crees v Royal London Insurance* (1996) that no further delay was possible. Mrs Crees was still ill at the end of the four week period and submitted a further medical certificate. As the claimant had not physically returned to work she had forfeited her right to return.

It was held by the EAT in *Lavery v Plessey Communications Ltd* (1982) that these notices must be strictly complied with, otherwise the employee loses her right to return.

Continuation of contract

The Court of Appeal held in *McKnight v Adlestones (Jewellers) Ltd* (1984) that where an employee fails to exercise her right to return to work in the proper manner, then the contract is automatically terminated, and the employee is not dismissed.

The new statutory right to 14 weeks' maternity leave now expressly stipulates that the contract is to remain in existence during that period.

The 14-week provision gives the employee an unconditional right to return to her original position. The only exception relates to a redundancy, and in that situation she must be offered any suitable alternative employment that is available. The 29-week entitlement, however, gives her the right to return to her original position, unless:

- it is not reasonably practical and she is offered suitable alternative employment;
- her employer has five employees or less and it is not reasonably practical to re-employ her.

Compulsory leave

There is a compulsory period of leave in the two weeks after childbirth during which the employer is not allowed to permit the employee to return to work.

When a woman has a contractual maternity entitlement giving her more money or more leave, she may exercise whichever of her contractual or statutory rights which are most beneficial to her – she may exercise a 'composite right' consisting of the most favourable aspects of any of her rights as opposed to being required to choose between one bundle of rights or another.

Time off provisions (ss 50–63 of the ERA 1996)

Employees have a statutory right to time off work for certain specified purposes. There is no continuous employment requirement for these, except for time off to seek work whilst under notice of redundancy where continuous employment of two years is necessary.

- Trade union duties (s 168 of the TULR(C)A)

  Trade union officials of independent-recognised trade unions have a right to a reasonable amount of paid time off in order to undertake union duties such as negotiation with the employer on matters for which the union is recognised and also for training for such duties. ACAS has issued a Code of Practice which gives examples of duties for which time off should be given, eg preparing for negotiation, consulting and reporting back to union members as well as actual negotiation on such matters as terms and conditions of employment, recruitment policies, redundancies, etc. The Code also suggests that an employer should release employees for initial basic training in industrial relations as soon as possible after they have been appointed.

They should be paid what they would have received had they worked normally during that time.

- Trade union activities (s 170 of the TULR(C)A)

  Trade union members of recognised independent trade unions are entitled to a reasonable amount of unpaid time off to take part in union activities. This does not include taking part in industrial action, neither does it cover such matters as lobbying parliament against proposed legislation.

- Safety representatives (Regulation 4 of the Safety Representative etc Regulations 1977 and Regulation 7 of the Health and Safety Regulations 1996)

  Safety representatives (whether appointed by a trade union or elected by the workforce) are entitled to as much paid time off as they need in order to undertake their duties and undergo relevant training. Candidates for election as an employee safety representative are entitled to reasonable (unpaid) time off.

- Elected employee representatives (for collective consultation purposes)

  Elected employee representatives are entitled to reasonable paid time off in order to perform their functions; and candidates for election as employee representatives are entitled to reasonable paid for the purpose.

- Public duties (s 50 of the ERA 1996)

  An employer must allow an employee a reasonable amount of unpaid time off to perform a specified range of public duties or attend meetings, eg Justices of the Peace, prison visitors, members of local authorities, statutory tribunals, police authorities, a relevant health or education body and the environment agency.

- Redundancies (s 52 of the ERA 1996)

  Employees under notice of redundancy are entitled to a reasonable paid time off to look for new work or to arrange training.

- Pregnancy (s 58 of the ERA 1996)

  Pregnant employees have a right to paid time off to receive antenatal care (for provisions on maternity leave see above).

Sunday working

The ERA, Part IV (incorporating the provisions of the Sunday Trading Act 1994) is designed to ensure that shop work on a Sunday is voluntary, except for those employed only to work on a Sunday. A shop worker is defined as 'anyone who is or may be required under their contract to do shop work, which is work in or about a shop'.

They are classified into:

- protected shop workers – who were employed before the provisions came into force and who are not required under the contract to work on a Sunday;

- opted out shop workers – who may be required under the contract to work on a Sunday, but have given three months' written notice to opt out.

It is automatically unfair to dismiss, or select for redundancy either category for refusing to work on a Sunday.

They must not be subjected to any detriment short of dismissal for refusing to work on a Sunday, eg disciplinary action or blocked promotion. (Financial incentives for those who work on a Sunday is not a detriment to those who do not.)

The employer must give new employees a statement of their rights to opt out within two months of starting work. Both protected shop workers and opted out shop workers may lose protection if they opt in, but may opt out again at a later date.

Directives to be implemented

Working Time Directive

New statutory restrictions on hours of work and rest periods will have to be introduced in order to comply with the EC Working Time Directive, which should have been implemented by November 1996. In the meantime, public sector workers can rely on the directive itself, and other workers may be able to sue the government (see Chapter 1). The UK government failed in its challenge to the directive on the ground that it should not have been brought in as a Health and Safety measure.

The directive provides for:

- A maximum working week of 48 hours a week, but exceptions can be made in the case of employees who volunteer to exceed the maximum. It does not in any case apply to jobs where working time is not measured.

- A minimum rest period of one day a week and 11 hours a day, and a rest break after six hours. Again, these do not apply where working time is not measured, or in jobs which require continuity of service, or shift work (except for rest breaks), or where there is a collective agreement to the contrary.

- Special protection for night workers, eg shifts averaging no more than eight hours, transfer to day work where possible if unfit to continue night work, free health checks and health and safety facilities equal to those available during the day. Same exclusions apply to some limits on shifts as apply to rest periods.

- Four weeks' minimum annual leave after 1999, three weeks until then, with no permitted exclusions.

Certain industries, eg transport, sea fishing, doctors in training are totally excluded. Certain types of workers can also be exempted from most of the provisions where they are not employed on fixed hours, eg managerial or professional jobs and family workers.

The Young Workers Directive

The Health and Safety (Young Persons) Regulations 1997 has partly implemented the provisions of this directive in so far as it refers to health and safety protection for young workers. They prevent an employer from employing a person under 18, unless he has first carried out a risk assessment. The employment of persons under school-leaving age is also prohibited in a number of specified circumstances. Further provisions governing the employment of adolescents (employees between 15 and 18) remain to be implemented, eg their entitlement to minimum breaks and rest periods; and a requirement that they be subject to a free assessment of their health capacities before they are assigned to regular night work.

Parental Leave Directive

This was introduced under the Social Chapter, which the UK is now joining.

The directive gives all workers an individual right to at least three months unpaid leave following the birth or adoption of a child. This right may be exercised at any time before the child's eighth birthday, and should be on a non-transferable basis, ie where both parents work, they should be entitled to three months leave each.

The directive also entitles workers to time off work on grounds of *force majeure* for urgent family reasons in cases of sickness or accident making the immediate presence of the worker indispensable.

4 Anti-discrimination legislation

You should be familiar with the following areas:

Legislation prohibiting discrimination on the ground of:
- Sex – the Sex Discrimination Act 1975 (as amended);
  the Equal Pay Act 1970 (as amended); Article 119 of the
  the Treaty of Rome; the Equal Pay Directive 75/117;
  the Equal Treatment Directive 76/207
- Marital status – the Sex Discrimination Act 1975;
  the Equal Treatment Directive 76/207
- Race, colour, nationality, ethnic origin, or national origin –
  the Race Relations Act 1976
- Disability – the Disability Discrimination Act 1995

Note

In most instances, decisions made by the courts under the Sex Discrimination Act (SDA) 1975 and under the Race Relations Act (RRA) 1976 are interchangeable and the same cases can be used, and are used, to interpret either act. The two Acts follow much the same pattern and use much the same terminology. Statements made with regard to the SDA will in general also apply to the RRA which will only be dealt with separately in so far as it differs from the SDA. A major difference is that the RRA is not subject to European law.

Discrimination on the grounds of sex

It is necessary to examine the relationship between different legislations in connection with sex discrimination.

Relationship between the Sex Discrimination Act and the Equal Pay Act

The Equal Pay Act (EPA) 1970 covers contractual rights, eg pay, holidays, fringe benefits; the SDA covers non-contractual rights; eg appointments, promotion, dismissal. They are mutually exclusive in their coverage and any action must be brought under the correct statute, but it has been said that they must be interpreted so as to form a 'harmonious code'.

The RRA covers both contractual and non-contractual matters.

Significance of EU legislation

It is important that students turn back to p 3, Chapter 1, at this stage to refresh their knowledge of the effect of EU law on domestic law.

The following EU legislation applies to this area:

- Article 119 Treaty of Rome

  This requires that men and women should receive equal pay for equal work. Pay is defined to cover pay or any other consideration whether in cash or in kind and whether received directly or indirectly.

- Equal Pay Directive 75/117

  This clarifies Article 119. It states that it requires equal pay to be paid for work of equal value. It also states that any job classification must be drawn up to exclude discrimination on grounds of sex.

- Equal Treatment Directive 76/207

  This requires the implementation of the principle of equal treatment for men and women in all aspects of employment.

Article 119 is directly effective. Directives are directly effective vertically but not horizontally. However, it has been suggested that since the Equal Pay Directive only explains the provisions of Article 119, and does not go beyond that, then it has the same effect as Article 119 itself.

If there is a remedy under English law, then that should be sought. But if a better remedy is available in European law then a claimant may base her claim on European law. She may take her claim to the European Court of Justice (ECJ) after she has exhausted the legal processes in the UK; or as is becoming increasingly common, the UK court may refer the matter for advice to the ECJ.

Sex Discrimination Act 1975

These provisions also apply to the RRA 1976, except for those matters separately considered on pp 89, 90.

Prohibited grounds

The SDA 1975 prohibits discrimination on the grounds of sex and marital status. Although expressed here in terms of discrimination against women, it applies equally to men and women. Indeed many of the cases brought under the SDA 1975 have been brought by men.

Kinds of discrimination

The Acts define three kinds of discrimination – direct discrimination, indirect discrimination and victimisation.

Direct discrimination

Direct discrimination is less favourable treatment on grounds of sex, marital status or race, etc.

There are two requirements:

- less favourable treatment;
- on the prohibited grounds.

Less favourable treatment

- *Sexual harassment*

    In *Porcelli v Strathclyde Regional Council* (1985) sexual harassment was held for the first time to amount to less favourable treatment and consequently to sex discrimination. Previous cases on sexual harassment had been based on constructive dismissal, but in this case the claimant lacked the necessary period of continuous employment, and so had to rely on the SDA 1975. A laboratory technician was driven into resigning by the campaign of unpleasantness conducted by her two male colleagues. They argued that they would have behaved in a similar way to a male colleague they disliked. It was held, however, that it amounted to sexual harassment because of the methods used and it resulted in less favourable treatment.

    Sexual harassment is defined by the European Commission in a Code of Practice as 'Conduct of a sexual nature, or other conduct based on sex affecting the dignity of men and women at work, including conduct of superior colleagues.'

In *Wileman v Miniec Engineering Ltd* (1988) a subjective test was used. What may be offensive to one person will not necessarily be offensive to another. A small amount of compensation was also issued because the claimant wore 'provocative clothes' and 'flaunted herself'.

In *Bracebridge Engineering v Darby* (1990) it was held that one incident could amount to sexual harassment. A failure by an employer to take a complaint seriously or to make a proper investigation would amount to a constructive dismissal.

It is for the tribunal to decide what amounts to less favourable treatment. In *Stewart v Cleveland Guest (Engineering) Ltd* (1994), the EAT refused to overturn a tribunal's decision that the employers had not discriminated against the complainant on grounds of sex by allowing male employees to display nude pinups in the workplace, although they knew that she found them offensive – on the ground that she had not suffered less favourable treatment.

In *de Souza v AA* (1986), the Court of Appeal stated that racial insults by themselves are not enough; they must also suggest to the reasonable worker that he had been disadvantaged in his work.

• *Dress and appearance*

Employers often require certain standards of dress from their employees whilst at work.

In *Schmidt v Austick Bookshop Ltd* (1977) the EAT held that it was not unlawful for an employer to dismiss a woman for wearing trousers at work as male employees were also subject to restrictions on what they could wear. There was no less favourable treatment. This ruling was confirmed by the Court of Appeal in *Smith v Safeway plc* (1996) where it declared not unlawful the dismissal of a man for having a ponytail. Men and women could be treated differently without this amounting to less favourable treatment, provided the rules required from all employees a conventional standard of appearance.

Prohibited grounds
Sex

This has previously been enforced by the courts in this country as a prohibition against discrimination on the ground of gender.

However, in *P v S* (1996) the ECJ held that the dismissal of a transsexual was covered by the Equal Treatment Directive. The court denied that the directive was confined to whether a person was of one sex or another, but was intended to cover any discrimination whatsoever on the grounds of sex.

Following this case, an industrial tribunal in *Grant v S West Transport Ltd* (1997) has asked the ECJ for a ruling on whether it is contrary to the Equal Treatment Directive or Article 119 for an employer to refuse travel concessions to the same sex partner of an employee, whereas the spouse or co-habitee of the opposite sex would have been granted the concessions. The Court of Appeal in *R v Ministry of Defence, ex p Perkins* (1997) has also referred to the ECJ the question whether the Equal Treatment Directive should be interpreted as including discrimination based on a persons sexual orientation, and if so, whether there could be an exception covering the need of the armed forces for effectiveness in war.

Pregnancy

There has been considerable controversy as to whether a refusal to employ or promote or to dismiss a woman on the grounds of pregnancy would amount to discrimination on the ground of sex.

First it was held not to be so, on the ground that there was no male equivalent (*Turley v Allders Department Store* (1980)). Then, the EAT decided that a pregnant woman could be compared to a man with a long-term health problem. But in *Dekker v VJU Centrum* (1991), a Dutch case, the ECJ ruled that a refusal to appoint a pregnant woman was direct sex discrimination, and contrary to the Equal Treatment Directive.

In *Webb v EMO Cargo* (1995), Webb was recruited to take over the work of a pregnant employee who was on maternity leave, but was to remain with the company afterwards (appointed for an indefinite period). She then discovered that she was pregnant and was dismissed. The case was referred to the ECJ by the House of Lords. The ECJ held that the dismissal amounted to direct sex discrimination. (*Note* – direct discrimination cannot be justified.) The House of Lords applied the ruling of the European Court. But Lord Keith went on to say that pregnancy would not necessarily be a relevant circumstance where a woman is refused employment for a fixed period during the whole of which her pregnancy makes her unavailable for work.

It will therefore be for industrial tribunals in future to explore the apparent difference between the effect of pregnancy in indefinite and fixed term employment. Since s 99 of the ERA 1996, which made it automatically unfair to dismiss on the ground of pregnancy, this problem will only arise in future in connection with recruitment or promotion or selection for training courses.

Note

1   Sex must be the reason for the less favourable treatment, but motive is not relevant

In *Peake v Automotive Products Ltd* (1978), Denning stated that allowing women to leave work five minutes before men were allowed to leave was not discriminatory, but was a matter of safety and chivalry. He accepted in a later case that this was wrong, but still tried to justify the decision on the *de minimis* principle.

In *Grieg v Community Industry* (1979), it was held that a good motive was not a defence. In that case two women were recruited as painters and decorators on a building site. One did not turn up on the first day, and the director sent the other woman home as he genuinely believed it would be unwise for her to be the only woman on the site.

In *James v Eastleigh Council* (1990), the House of Lords held – by a bare majority – that the council was discriminatory in allowing free entry to a swimming pool to Mrs James who was 61, but also required Mr James who was also 61 to pay the full fee. The council did not intend to discriminate but wished to give concessions to pensioners. The House of Lords affirmed that the test for discrimination is objective (the 'but for' test) and that motive is irrelevant. The state retirement age is itself discriminatory and to base the concessions on that is also discriminatory.

But see *Dhatt v McDonalds Hamburger Ltd* (1991), where an Indian was asked to provide a work permit. This would not have been required of a UK or EC applicant. The Court of Appeal held that this request was not based on discrimination but on the immigration legislation of the UK government. The 'but for' rule was not applied in this case.

2   The right to discriminate cannot be purchased

In *Ministry of Defence v Jeremiah* (1980), men who volunteered for overtime were required to work in dirty conditions in the 'colour-bursting shop', but this would not apply to women as it would affect their hair. It was held that this was discriminatory despite the fact that men were paid extra 'obnoxious' money.

3   Employers must not rely on 'stereotypes'

In *Coleman v Skyrail Oceanic Ltd* (1981), Mrs Coleman was dismissed when she married an employee from a rival firm. On the ground that she might give away confidential information (which she had not done during her engagement) and that her husband was the breadwinner. The Court of Appeal held that the dismissal was discriminatory – on the ground that the assumption that the man was the breadwinner without any investigation was itself discriminatory.

In *Horsey v Dyfed CC* (1982) it was held discriminatory to refuse a request for social work training on the ground that at the end of the training period the applicant would stay in London where her husband worked, rather than return to Wales. Again the council had relied on stereotypical views, instead of investigating the actual circumstances. The EAT did not say that an employer could never act on the basis that a woman would give up her job to follow her husband. What the employer could not do was assume that she would do so.

Marital status
There is no prohibition against a person being discriminated against because he or she is single.

Indirect discrimination
Judicial recognition of 'indirect' or adverse impact' discrimination can be traced to the US Supreme Court ruling in *Griggs v Duke Power Co* (1971) where certain aptitude tests were held to be discriminatory. It has been described as involuntary, or hidden, or institutional discrimination, where tests or requirements which are applied to both sexes in fact discriminate against one sex.

It occurs when:

1   An employer imposes a requirement or condition.

    The requirement or condition:

    * May be precisely defined as in *Price v Civil Service* (1979), where the applicant had to be under 28 years of age; or it can be a number of 'vague factors' as in *Clarke v Eley Kynoch Ltd* (1982), as long as they must be complied with.

    * Must be a total bar to the job. In *Perera v Civil Service Commission* (1983), the applicant complained that the respondents took into account practical experience in England and the ability to communicate in English into their consideration of applicants for administrative trainees. It was held that these were not requirements or conditions, but merely some of the plus and minus factors which employers took into consideration.

However in *Enderby v Frenchay AHA* (1991) (see p 85), the ECJ held that where a case is being brought directly under Article 119, a 'requirement' is not necessary. But it was held in *Bhudi v IMI Refiners Ltd* (1994) that it remains necessary for cases brought under the SDA. This has been criticised on the grounds that it allows employers to evade the effect of the Act by substituting criteria for requirements.

2   The applicant is unable to comply with the requirement or condition. The courts have held that 'can comply' does not necessarily mean 'can physically comply'. In *Mandla v Dowell Lee* (1983), a case involving a Sikh's refusal to cut his hair, the House of Lords understood 'can comply' to mean 'can comply consistently with the customs and cultural conditions of the racial group', rather than 'can physically perform'.

In *Price v Civil Service Commission* (1978), the EAT thought that the phrase was to be interpreted broadly. 'It should not be said that because it was theoretically possible for someone to do something, that he can do it in practice.' Mrs Price who was 36, sought to become an executive officer in the Civil Service, but her application was rejected because the employers sought candidates between the ages of 17 and 28. The reason why she had not applied within that age group was because she had two small children and she argued that this was the position of many women, so considerably fewer could qualify for the job. The industrial tribunal rejected the application on the ground that the number of men and women in the relevant age group was the same, and since no-one is obliged to have children, the applicant could have complied with the condition. The case was sent back by the EAT with instructions to examine 'current usual behaviour', and 'general social facts'. In fact the respondents then conceded that the number of women who could comply with the conditions were much less than the number of men. They failed to justify the practice, since it was too wide and discriminatory a way of achieving the aim of the Civil Service to retain a proper career structure.

3   A considerably smaller proportion of the applicant's group can comply with the requirement.

   • The Court of Appeal has held that this is a question of fact for the tribunal to decide.

   • It is important to bring statistical evidence to show 'that a considerably smaller proportion can comply'.

      In *Clarke v Eley Kynoch Ltd* (1982), where the dismissal of part-time workers in a redundancy was held to be discriminatory, it had been shown that 100% of the part-time workers in that organisation were women, and that 80% of part-time workers nationally are women.

But in *Kidd v DRG Ltd* (1985), no statistics were quoted by the claimant. The tribunal held that it is not safe to assume that a greater proportion of women than men or married women than unmarried women took on a child caring role. The EAT agreed that it was right for the tribunal to reject 'generalised assumptions'.

• The correct pool must be selected for comparison.

In *Jones v Manchester University* (1993), the university advertised for a graduate aged between 27–35 years of age. Miss Jones, aged 46, and otherwise well-qualified for the post was not short-listed. Miss Jones had qualified as a mature student and as there were more female than male mature students, more female students would be debarred from applying for the post. The Court of Appeal, however, held that the correct pool in this case was all graduates not only those who graduated as mature students, and warned against choosing a pool in a way that manipulated the result.

In *R v Secretary of State for Employment, ex p EOC* (1995), the correct pool was held to be all part-time workers in the country.

• There is no specific meaning for 'considerably smaller' in the Sex Discrimination Act.

However, in *R v Secretary of State for Employment, ex p Seymour Smith* (1995), the Court of Appeal found that the proportion of women who could meet the two-year qualifying period for unfair dismissal claims was 90% of the proportion of men. This was found to be sufficient under the Equal Treatment Directive and gave rise to a presumption of indirect discrimination which was for the government to justify.

The court stated that the weight attached to 'considerable' should not be exaggerated.

cf – USA where the phrase means 80%.

4 The requirement cannot be justified.

In *Steel v UPOW* (1977), the court stated that the tribunal in considering justification had to weigh up the needs of the enterprise against the discriminatory effect of the requirement or condition. The tribunal must be satisfied that the requirement is necessary, not merely convenient. Further, it must consider whether there was a non-discriminatory method of achieving the same end.

However, the requirement was later diluted: in *Singh v Rowntree* (1979), it was stated that the requirement must be 'reasonable'. In *Ojutiku v MSC* (1982) the requirement 'should seem sound and tolerable to right thinking people'.

In *Hampson v DES* (1989), the House of Lords held that the employer must show a 'real necessity' for the requirement, be it economic or administrative efficiency and that a balance be struck between the discriminatory effect of the requirement or condition, and the needs of the person who applies it.

It followed the ruling of the ECJ in *Bilka-Kaufhaus v Weber Von Herz* (1986), where it was stated that in order to justify a requirement, it had to be shown that the requirement:

- corresponded to a real need on the part of the undertaking;
- was appropriate for achieving that end; and
- was necessary for achieving that end.

Lord Keith stated in *Rainey v Greater Glasgow Health Board* (1987) (see below p 85) that justification under the Sex Discrimination Act has now, therefore, been brought into line with justification under European law and also the defence of 'material difference' under The Equal Pay Act 1970, but it is not clear that the rule laid down in *Hampson* is identical with that in Bilka-Kaufhause.

Victimisation

Victimisation occurs where a person is treated less favourably because he brings or has brought proceedings given evidence or information or alleged a contravention of the SDA, the EPA or the RRA.

Victimisation has proved difficult to establish in practice.

In *Aziz v Trinity Taxis Ltd* (1988), Aziz was expelled from an association of taxi drivers for having made a secret tape recording with a view to obtaining proof of discriminatory practices. The respondents successfully argued that any individual who had breached confidentiality in the same way would have been expelled. To amount to victimisation, the applicant must have been dismissed for one of the matters set out in the Act.

Similarly in *Nagaraian v Agnew* (1995), it was held the protection was confined to events occurring during employment and would not cover a reference written after the employee has left.

However, in *Northants CC v Dattani* (1994), halting internal investigation into an allegation of racial discrimination when the employee commenced a tribunal claim was held to be victimisation.

Discrimination in employment

The Act covers not only employees, but anyone working personally. Since the protection is not dependent on a contract of employment, the EAT held in *Leighton v Michael* (1996) that an employee may bring a claim of discrimination even though her contract is unenforceable because it is tainted with illegality.

Section 1 covers:

* Arrangements for selecting employees and the making of an offer of employment.

  In *Saunders v Richmond BC* (1977), a woman who applied for a job as a golf professional was asked certain questions such as how she thought a man might take to being instructed by a woman. It was held that these questions were pertinent to the job and not discriminatory.

  In the EOC Code of Practice, employers are advised not to ask questions about marriage or family intentions.

* The terms upon which employment is offered. (The terms themselves when employment has been obtained will be covered by the EPA.)

* Refusing or omitting to offer employment.

Section 2 covers:

* Access to promotion or training

  See *Horsey v Dyfed CC* (above, p 69).

* Dismissal, or any other detriment.

  See *MOD v Jeremiah* (above, p 68).

  In *Porcelli v Strathclyde* (1986), sexual harassment *per se* was held to be a detriment. But in *De Souza v AA* (1986) racial insults by themselves were held not to amount to a detriment.

Exceptions

* The provisions of the Act do not apply to special treatment afforded to women in connection with pregnancy or childbirth.

- The Act stated that it did not apply to provisions relating to death or retirement, but this has been overruled by the ECJ in *Marshall v Southampton and West Hampshire Health Authority* and *Barber v Royal Exchange Ass Group* (see below, p 88).
- Health and safety requirements.
- Miscellaneous matters

  (a) Police, Prison Officers, Clergy (ss 17–21)

  (b) Necessity of complying with statutory requirements (s 51)

  (c) National Security (s 52)

- Positive action (s 48)

  Where in the previous year there were no, or few, members of one sex doing a particular job, an employer may:

  (a) encourage women to take advantage of opportunities for doing that work;

  (b) afford women only 'access to facilities for training' to help fit them for doing that work.

These are the only positive actions allowed by the Act.

The ECJ ruled in *Kalanke v Freie Hansestadt Bremen* (1996) that positive discrimination is also contrary to European law.

Genuine occupational qualifications

These apply only to recruitment, transfers and training.

They do not apply to the terms upon which employment is offered, dismissal or subjecting a person to a detriment.

Neither do they apply where the employer already has a sufficient number of suitable employees to carry out the duties.

The sex of a person is a 'genuine occupational qualification' in the following circumstances:

- where the nature of the job calls for authentic male or female characteristics (excluding physical strength or stamina); eg actors, models;
- where the job needs to be held by a man or a woman in order to preserve decency or privacy because it is likely to involve physical contact, or because persons are in a state of undress, or using sanitary facilities.

  In *Wylie v Dee & Co* (1978) a tribunal held it was wrong to turn down a woman applicant for a job as sales assistant in a menswear shop, as there were plenty of other employees in the shop who could take inside leg measurements.

- the employee is required to live in premises provided by the employer, which are not equipped with separate sleeping accommodation, or sanitary facilities and it would be unreasonable to expect the employer to provide theses items;
- the job is in a single sex establishment such as a prison, a hospital or other establishment for people who need special care and it is reasonable that the job should be held by a person of a particular sex;
- the holder of the job provides people with personal services, promoting their welfare or education, which can most effectively be provided by a person of a particular sex;

In *Times v Hodgson* (1981), a male supervisor was chosen for redundancy ahead of the only female supervisor, as the employer wished to retain one female to deal with the problems of female workers, eg to take them to the first aid room, etc.

But in *London Borough of Lambeth v CRE* (1990) the Court of Appeal held that personal service must involve personal contact and an administrative post such as housing manager would not qualify.

- the job needs to be held by a man because of the restrictions imposed by laws regulating the employment of women;
- the job is likely to involve foreign service in a country with laws regulating the employment of women;
- the job is one of two to be held by a married couple;
- The job involves living or working in a private home and involves intimate physical or social contact.

Other forms of employment discrimination (ss 11–15)

In addition to discrimination in 'employment', other types of discrimination is made unlawful, eg discrimination against 'contract workers', discrimination by trade unions, partnerships, qualifying bodies, vocational training bodies and employment agencies.

Other unlawful Acts (s 41)

- It is unlawful to give instructions to discriminate or to offer any benefits to induce such discrimination.
- An Act done by an employee 'in the course of his employment' shall be treated as having been done by the employer, whether or

not it was done with his approval, unless he can show that he took such steps as were reasonably practical to prevent the employee from doing the act.

In *Tower Boot Co v Jones* (1997) the Court of Appeal held that the phrase 'in the course of employment' should be interpreted broadly without reference to its meaning at common law. A coloured 16-year-old had left the company after one month because he had been physically assaulted and verbally abused by his fellow workers. His arm had been burnt with a hot screw-driver, metal bolts were thrown at his head, his legs had been whipped, he was called 'chimp', 'monkey' and 'baboon'. The EAT decided that this behaviour could not be treated as done 'in the course of employment' as they could not be described as improper modes of performing authorised tasks. The Court of Appeal reversed the decision.

In *Burton v Rhule and De Vere Hotels* (1996), the EAT decided that an employer subjects an employee to racial harassment where the harassment is inflicted by a third party (Bernard Manning) and where the employer could have put a stop to the harassment or reduced the extent of it.

Employment advertisements

It is also unlawful to advertise in such a manner as to indicate an intention to discriminate and the use of a job description in advertisements with a sexual connotation such as a 'waiter', 'postman' will be assumed to be discriminatory unless the advertisement contains an indication to the contrary. It is the EOC alone which can take action in this connection. The EOC has issued a document called 'Guidance on Employment Advertising' containing useful advice.

Enforcement

An individual must bring a claim within three months of the discrimination, unless the tribunal considers it 'just and equitable' to extend the time. Tribunals have been instructed to apply this in a liberal fashion.

The three months run from the last act of discrimination. An act which continues over a period is deemed to have been performed at the end of the period (*Barclays Bank v Kapur* (1991)). A distinction must be made, however, between a continuing act and an act which has continuing consequences, eg a failure to appoint a person to a particular post.

Burden of proof

Lord Wedderburn has pointed out that law in action depends more often than not on burdens of proof and procedures.

The burden of proof is on the individual alleging the discrimination. This poses great difficulty, especially in cases involving a failure to hire or to promote – where most complaints arise.

There have been arguments over whether the burden of proof moves, once a *prima facie* case of discrimination has been established. In *King v Britain China Centre* (1991), the Court of Appeal ruled that there could be no formal reversal of the burden of proof, but because it was unusual to find direct evidence of discrimination, a tribunal is entitled to draw an inference from the primary facts. If, for instance, a person from a different race seems to have been treated differently, then the tribunal may deduce that this was because of racial discrimination unless the employer can provide a convincing explanation. Under US law, once the applicant has shown that she has the necessary minimum qualification, it is for the employer to show that she was less qualified than the appointee.

A directive on the burden of proof is currently under discussion at the European Union.

Questionnaires

In an attempt to help with the proof of discrimination, the claimant may submit a questionnaire to the employer asking if he discriminates! If he says no, further information may be requested. Although adverse inferences may be drawn if the employer refuses to answer, or is evasive, the procedure does nor seem particularly helpful in practice, and may in fact lead to a premature disclosure of the applicants case to the employer.

Statistics

Statistical evidence may be important both for direct and indirect discrimination.

In *West Midland Passenger Transport v Singh* (1988) the claimant sought statistics relating to the ethnic origin of applicants for promotion and the ethnic origin of those who were successful and these were considered by the tribunal, and contributed to the success of his claim. It was pointed out that the CRE Code of Practice recommended ethnic monitoring and employers also used evidence of this sort to disprove discrimination. However, if employers do not monitor, then statistical evidence will not be available.

Discovery of documents

Proving discrimination may be impossible without access of documents which the employer holds, eg qualification, references, etc. Since these are confidential, the applicant will not have access to them unless discovery is ordered.

In *Nasse v SRC* (1979), the Court of Appeal held that an industrial tribunal should not order the disclosure of a reference given in confidence except in rare cases, where after inspection of the documents, the chairman decides that it is essential in the interests of justice that the confidence should be overridden.

Remedies

- An order declaring the rights of the parties.
- An order requiring the respondents to pay damages.

Originally, a limit was placed on the amount of damages payable. However, in *Marshall v SW Hants AHA (No 2)* (1993), the ECJ declared that such a limit was contrary to the Equal Treatment Directive which required claimants to be compensated in full. This was only effective vertically against emanations of the state.

The limit was removed for all claimants under the SDA by the Sex Discrimination and Equal Pay Regulations 1993 and for claimants under the RRA by the Race Relations (Remedies) Act 1994.

The effect of this change has been dramatic, as seen from damages of up to £300,000 awarded against the Ministry of Defence in a sequence of cases arising from the dismissal of pregnant servicewomen.

The Court of Appeal enunciated the following principles for assessing damages in *Alexander v The Home Office* (1988):

1 The object of damages is restitution. It should not be minimal, because this trivialises and diminishes public respect for the policy behind the act; excessive awards could have the same effect and given the impossibility of precise quantification, awards should be restrained.

2 Damages can be awarded for injury to feelings, but injury to feelings is of shorter duration than physical injury. Such damages however can be substantial as in *HM Prison v Jonson* (1997), where damages of £21,000 for injured feelings were awarded to a black prison warder who had had to suffer racial abuse over an extended period.

3 The conduct, character and circumstances of the claimant must be taken into account.

Note
Damages were not originally available for indirect discrimination, unless discrimination was intended. This was again altered to comply with European law. Regulations now allow the tribunal to award damages where it would be just and equitable to do so.

The law has not been changed with regard to race relations, but in *London Underground v Edwards* (1995) the EAT declared that an intention to discriminate could be inferred if an employer had imposed a requirement knowing it would disadvantage women. Presumably the same reasoning could be applied to indirect discrimination under the RRA 1976.

- A recommendation of action to be taken by the respondent to reduce the adverse effect of discrimination – eg *Price v Civil Service Commission* (above). However, it was held by the Court of Appeal in *NW Thames AHA v Noone* (above) that the employer could not be ordered to offer the applicant the next vacancy as the AHA was required by law to advertise all vacancies.

The EAT relied on the above decision in *British Gas v Sharma* (1991) to hold that they did not have the power to order that the applicant be promoted when the next vacancy arose, although there was no such legal requirement to advertise in the case of *British Gas*. If the employer does not comply with a recommendation, then additional compensation can be ordered.

The Equal Opportunities Commission

For the duties and function of the EOC, turn to Chapter 1, p 12.

Equal Pay Act 1970 (as amended)

The EPA 1970 is concerned with the establishment of equal terms and conditions of employment for men and women. The Act provides that the contract of employment of all women is deemed to include an equality clause, which will operate whenever a woman is employed on *like work* with a man, or on work which is *rated equivalent*, or on *work of equal value*.

If a claim is upheld, the industrial tribunal may also award damages which represent arrears of pay of up to two years. (*Note* – it has been suggested that the limit of two years may conflict with European law and the matter has been referred to the ECJ.)

The EPA 1970 is subject to the overriding effect of Article 119 of the Treaty of Rome, and the Equal Pay Directive 75/115.

Disputes on equal pay can be brought directly under these provisions, claims brought under the national legislation must be interpreted in the light of European legislation, and disputes can be referred for a final decision to the European Court of Justice.

The comparator

The comparator must be in the 'same employment' as the applicant, ie must be employed by her employer or an associated employer at the same establishment or at another establishment which has common terms and conditions of employment.

* Associated employer

  Employers are 'associated' under the Act if one is a company of which the other (directly or indirectly) has control, or both are companies of which a third person (directly or indirectly) has control.

  In *Scullard v Knowles* (1996) the EAT held that this definition excluded employers who were not companies. However, it also pointed out that Article 119 does not require an employer to be a company and that the ECJ has stated that it applies where men and women work in the 'same establishment or service, whether private or public'.

* Common terms and conditions

  In *Leverton v Clwyd CC* (1989), a nursery nurse claimed parity with clerical staff employed by the council at a different establishment. The council had concluded a comprehensive collective agreement with NALGO (the purple book) covering all staff and containing six separate pay scales. The House of Lords concluded that this was a situation where there were common terms and conditions for all staff.

  In *British Coal Corporation v Smith* (1994) the Court of Appeal explained that 'common terms and conditions' must be those of men working at the women's establishment, or which would be available for male employees at the women's establishment if there were any.

* The complainant may choose the man with whom she wishes to be compared and the tribunal may not substitute another man whom it considers more appropriate.

- Multiple comparators are allowed.
- In *Macarthys v Smith* (1979) the European Court of Justice held that a woman could use a former employee as comparator.
- The appellant cannot choose a hypothetical comparator.

Like work

In order to determine whether a woman is employed on 'Like Work', the Act provides that:

- The work must be the 'same or broadly similar' and any differences between the work done is not of practical importance.

  In *Capper Pass v Lawton* (1977) the EAT upheld a decision that a woman who worked as a cook in the directors dining room was entitled to equal pay with the two assistant chefs who worked in the works canteen.

- If there are differences between the work done, the tribunal must ask whether they are such that it is reasonable to see them reflected in the wage settlement. Would two men doing those jobs be paid differently?

  In *Noble v David Gold & Son Ltd* (1980), the men worked in a warehouse loading and unloading, whereas the women did lighter work, such as sorting and packing. Held: not on 'like work'.

- Regard must be had to what happens in practice. Are any additional duties in a man's contract of employment spurious?

  In *Electrolux v Hutchinson* (1976), more highly-paid men performed the same work as women but their contracts included a flexibility clause and a commitment to overtime. However, the EAT discovered that they had not actually been required to fulfil these duties and held that they were on 'like work' with the women.

- The time at which work is done is not necessarily significant.

  In *Dugdale v Kraft Foods Ltd* (1977) men and women worked on 'like work' but the men worked night shifts and the women worked during the day. It was held that the hours at which work is performed is by itself no bar to equal pay at the basic rate – the men could be compensated by an unsocial hours premium.

  However, in *Thomas v NCB* (1987) it was held that a male canteen assistant, working on his own, unsupervised, at night, was not on 'like work' with canteen assistants who worked during the day under supervision.

Work rated as equivalent

A woman's work will be considered to have been rated equivalent to that of a man if it had been given equal value under a properly conducted job evaluation scheme, eg in terms of effort, skill, decisions, etc.

In *Eaton v Nuttal* (1977), it was said that the scheme had to be 'thorough in analysis and capable of impartial application'.

To qualify, the JES:

* must be analytical.

  In *Bromley v Quick* (1988), it was held that it must contain an accurate job description and criteria against which each job is measured. A subjective job evaluation would not suffice.

* Must have been accepted as accurate by the parties who commissioned it – generally the employer and a trade union.

Once both parties have accepted the validity of the scheme, it must be put into force.

In *O'Brian v Sim-Chem Ltd* (1980), a JES was carried out, but before it was put into operation, the government announced a voluntary incomes policy. The House of Lords held that once the scheme had been completed, the equality clause was to operate.

Work of equal value

The original Act only provided for equal pay for 'like work' or 'work rated as equivalent'. Following the decision of the ECJ in *Commission of the European Communities v UK* (1982) that the Act did not fully comply with the principle of 'Equal Pay for Equal Work', the government introduced the Equal Pay Amendment Regulations 1983 which provided a third ground upon which a woman could claim equal pay, that is her work is of equal value to that of a man. The Regulations came into force on 1 January 1984.

They provide as follows:

1 An equality clause is to be implied into a woman's contract of employment where a woman is employed on work which in terms of demand made upon her (for instance under such headings as effort, skill and decision making) is of equal value to those of a man in the same employment.

2 A woman may only claim under the Regulations if it is not work to which either of the first two situations apply. But there is no such limitation either in s 119 or the directive.

In *Pickstone v Freemans plc* (1988) the applicant was a warehouse operative who worked alongside male warehouse operatives and received the same pay. She brought an equal value claim naming as her comparator a male checker warehouse operator who was paid at a higher rate. Held: she was entitled to do this under the Treaty of Rome.

3   A woman will be allowed to pursue an 'Equal Value' claim even if her job and that of her male comparator are already covered by a JES provided she can show that the system used to measure the jobs clearly and manifestly discriminated on grounds of sex.

Procedures in an equal value claim

- If the claimant was not already covered by a JES scheme which is not 'clearly and manifestly discriminatory' then the tribunal can proceed with the claim as long as the JES was completed before the hearing (*Dibro v Hore* (1990)).

- The tribunal can refuse to proceed if the claim clearly has no hope of success.

- If the employer proves a 'material difference or material factor' defence, (see below) which must be pursued at this stage, then the tribunal cannot proceed with the claim. If considered at this stage, then it cannot be considered later. In the absence of any of the above, and if the applicant has established reasonable grounds for determining that the work is of equal value, the tribunal must proceed. Since 1996, the tribunal has a discretion as to whether it will refer the matter to an expert drawn from a list of suitable persons held by ACAS, or deal with the matter itself.

If referred to an expert:

- The expert will examine the jobs in question, hear representations, and report to the tribunal.

- The tribunal can accept the report, reject it, or commission a further report.

- Once the tribunal accepts a report, it automatically becomes evidence on the question of equal value.

Material difference and material factor

Even though a woman can show she is employed on 'like work' or 'work rated as equivalent', the employer may still be able to defend an equal pay claim by showing that the variation in was due to a 'material difference other than sex'. The burden of proof in this case is on the employer and his defence may include such matters as difference in length of service, a merit-grading scheme, better qualifications, better skill, different status, a night work premium, additional responsibility allowance, etc.

A new defence was introduced for employers in 'equal value' claims – he may show that the difference in pay is due to a 'Material factor, other than sex'. This change was apparently calculated to widen the scope of the employers defence, to include non-personal matters. However, both defences are governed by European law, and since *Rainey v Greater Glasgow Health Authority* (see below p 85) both are seen to operate in a very similar way.

The EOC's Code of Practice on Equal Pay which came into force in March 1970 states that the material factor defence is the 'reason put forward by the employer to explain why the comparator, although doing equal work, is paid more than the applicant'.

Scope of material difference and material factor defence

In *Tyldesley v TML Plastics Ltd* (1996), the EAT held that a genuine material factor defence can be established if the employer can show that the difference in pay is due to a genuine material factor which is not sex. There is no additional requirement to show that the difference is objectively justified unless it adversely impacts on women as a group. In that case the comparator was paid more than the claimant because he had more experience in total management skills. It was not necessary to show a real need for people with those skills. 'The EPA 1970 is about eliminating sex discrimination, not achieving fair wages'.

The same principle was applied by the Court of Session in Scotland in *Strathclyde Regional Council v Wallace* (1996) where female teachers who were carrying out the duties of principal teachers without being formally appointed to that position were paid less than formally appointed principal teachers. The court held that an objective justification for that practice was not necessary. The applicants have appealed to the House of Lords.

Where, however, the difference is itself tainted by sex in that it effects a considerably higher proportion of women than men, ie it has an adverse impact, then it must be objectively justified.

The ECJ ruled in the *Danfoss* case (1991) that where an undertaking applied a system of pay which was characterised by a lack of transparency and a female worker establishes that the average pay of the female is lower than that of the male workers. The burden of proof is on the employer to show that his pay practice is not discriminatory.

In *Bilka-Kaufhause v Weber von Harz* (1986), the ECJ held that in such circumstances the defence will only succeed, if the employer can show that:

- there was a real need for the provision;
- it was suitable for satisfying that need;
- it was necessary for that end.

Where there was an adverse impact, The House of Lords also in *Rainey v Greater Glasgow Health Board*, below, required the material factor to be objectively justified.

Examples of material differences or material factors

Market forces
In *Clay Cross (Quarry Services) Ltd v Fletcher* (1979), a woman was employed as a sales clerk at £35 a week. A colleague left and was replaced by a male employee who was paid £43 a week – the sum he was already earning in another job. The Court of Appeal held that 'market forces' which led to the unequal pay was no excuse.

However, this was overruled in *Rainey v Greater Glasgow Health Board* (1988), where a health authority decided to set up its own prosthetic service. The rates of pay for qualified prosthetists was on the same scale as medical physics technicians. However, in order to attract a sufficient number of qualified persons to get the service started, it was necessary to make a higher pay offer to those who came from the private sector. The applicant who came from the health service sought equal pay with a man on a higher salary who came from the private sector. Held: the difference in pay was due to a genuine material difference other than sex and this could be objectively justified by the needs of the employer. The House of Lords thought that the decision in Clay Cross was unduly restrictive, as economic grounds, objectively justified and also economic convenience were both capable of being genuine material differences other than sex.

In *Benveniste v Southampton University* (1989), it was held that although the defence applied when a woman lecturer was taken on at a low salary due to financial problems at the university, the defence would cease to apply when the University's financial problems were over.

The proportionality test
The extent of the market forces defence was considered by the ECJ in *Enderby v Frenchay Health Authority* (1993). In that case senior speech therapists employed by the Health Authority, claimed their work was of equal value with male principal pharmacists, and male clinical

psychologists, whose salaries exceeded theirs by up to 60%. The claimants pointed out that speech therapists were predominantly female whereas the comparator professions were predominantly male, and that this was the real reason why speech therapists were paid less. The employers argued that an overall shortage of applicants to the other professions meant that higher salaries had to be offered. It was accepted, however, that this would not account for all the difference. While accepting that market forces could constitute a genuine material difference, the ECJ indicated that the defence would only hold good for such part of the difference as could be attributed to that reason.

A further decision which limits the market forces defend is found in *Ratcliff v N Yorkshire CC* (1995), where the council's direct service organisation cut the pay of a group of employees in order to enable it to place in a low bid to carry out work which was subject to competitive tendering. The House of Lords held that 'although conscious of the difficult problem facing employers in seeking to compete with a rival tenderer ... to reduce women's wages below those of their male comparators was the very kind of discrimination which the Act tried to remove'. It was also stated that the distinction between direct and indirect discrimination with the possibility of justifying the latter, could not be imported from the SDA 1975 into the EPA 1970.

Collective bargaining

In *Enderby v Frenchay* (above) another argument put forward by the employer was that the pay structure in each case resulted from free collective bargaining, and that this constituted sufficient justification. The ECJ held that this was not an acceptable reason – separate collective bargaining may explain the difference, but does not justify it. This was also subsequently rejected as a defence by the Court of Appeal in *British Coal Corp v Smith* (1994) – a case involving mineworkers and catering staff.

Red circling

Problems have arisen with regard to 'red circling', ie where an employee is redundant, but is offered lower graded work but at his existing rate of pay. Such protected salary or 'red circling' may be challenged by women workers who are doing the same work but are paid the lower salary. The 'red circling' may be accepted as a 'genuine material difference' provided it is not the result of past discrimination, and providing it is phased out as soon as possible.

In *Snoxell v Vauxhall Motors* (1977), the company had different rates of pay for men and women doing the same job. On the EPA 1970 coming into force, the women's rate was established as the rate for the job, but the men previously employed were 'red circled' at their previous rate. Held: this was merely repeating past discrimination and was therefore no defence. (The company did not in any case have a plan to phase out the red circling.)

Part-time work
In *Jenkins v Kingsgate* (1981), the ECJ held that the fact that a man worked full time and a woman worked part time could constitute a 'genuine material difference, provided that it was not merely an indirect way of reducing the pay of part-time workers who were predominantly or wholly women. Any variation between the pay of full-time men and part-time women would have to be justified by reference to some non-discriminatory object.

This was also emphasised by the ECJ in *Bilke-Kaufhause v Weber von Herz* (see above). The ECJ declared that certain state provisions in Germany disqualifying part-time workers from sick pay schemes or redundancy schemes were unlawful. This led to *R v The Secretary of State for Employment, ex p EOC* (1994), where the qualifying hours for redundancy payments and unfair dismissal were also held to be unlawful by the House of Lords.

Performance related pay
In the *Danfoss* case above; the ECJ considered criteria which have a discriminatory effect, eg flexibility, which would need to be justified. They also stated that clear criteria should be adopted and applied objectively; and that a discriminatory impact should be examined and justified where necessary.

Note
In *Leverton v Clwyd* (above), the wide difference in the parties conditions of work were held to be a 'material difference'.

Remedies

If the tribunal finds in favour of the claimant, it will make an award of damages or arrears of pay which can be back dated for up to two years. The EAT in *Levez v Jennings Ltd* (1996) has referred the question whether this two-year limitation is compatible with European law to the ECJ.

What must be equalised?
In *Hayward v Cammell Laird Shipbuilders Ltd* (1988), the applicant joined Cammel Laird as a catering trainee. During the first three years she was

paid the same rate as apprentice painters, insulation engineers, and joiners, but thereafter she was paid at a lower rate. However, she enjoyed supervisor sickness benefits, paid meal breaks and extra holidays. Her claim for equal value was referred to an independent consultant who evaluated the jobs under the headings of:

• physical demands;

• environment considerations;

• skill and knowledge;

• planning and decision-making;

• responsibility.

He found the work of the applicant was of equal value with that of the three male comparators. The industrial tribunal, however, dismissed the claim – her terms and conditions as a whole (not just the cash pay) were not less favourable. The House of Lords reversed this decision – the basic salary of the applicant should not be less favourable than that of her comparators.

This approach was approved by the ECJ in *Barber v Guardian Royal Exchange* (1991).

Pensions

Pay has been interpreted very widely under Article 119 (see p 93). This has been particularly significant with regard to pensions.

Equality of retirement age was established in *Marshall v Southampton AHA* (1986); access to occupational pension schemes by part-timers in *Bilke-Kaufhaus GmbH v Weber von Hartz* (1987); age entitlement to pensions and pension benefits in *Barber v Royal Guardian Exchange* (1991). Mr Barber had been made redundant at the age of 52. Under the provisions of his non-contributory pension scheme, a man, if made redundant before the age of 62, could claim an immediate pension at 55. Women, however, if redundant, could claim a pension at 50. Mr Barber alleged sex discrimination, but, under the SDA 1975 as it then was, retirement and pension provisions were exempted from its operation. The Court of Appeal asked the ECR to give a preliminary ruling on whether a pension payable under a redundancy scheme could be 'pay' within the meaning of Article 119. The ECJ gave the following ruling:

• Benefits paid to an employee under a compulsory redundancy constitutes pay under Article 119.

• Private pensions are pay. It is contrary to Article 119 for a man to be entitled to a deferred pension and a woman to be entitled to an immediate pension.

- The direct effect of Article 119 on entitlement to pensions may not be relied on for entitlement prior to 17 May 1990, unless legal proceeding had already been instigated.

Subsequent cases have explained and interpreted further the full effects of *Barber*.

In *Smith v Advel Systems* (1994), the ECJ held that levelling down is not discriminatory.

Pensions are now covered by the Pensions Act 1995 and the Occupational Pension Schemes (Equal Treatment) Regulations 1995 which provide both for equal access to schemes but also for equal treatment during membership. Claims for equal treatment in pension schemes are to be brought under the EPA 1995, and must be made during the relevant employment or within six months afterwards. If such claims are successful, the employer must provide the resources necessary to secure the applicants accrued rights.

Note
It remains lawful to discriminate between men and women in relation to bridging pensions in order to compensate for the fact that men are entitled to a state pension at a later age than women; and also in the use of sex-related factors when calculating employers' contributions or determining certain benefits.

The Race Relations Act 1976

The RRA 1976 is similar in form and content to the SDA 1975 on which it was based. The cases which have been used to interpret the SDA also apply in most cases to the RRA, but there are certain differences.

The RRA:

- covers contractual and non-contractual matters;
- prohibits discrimination on grounds of 'colour, race, nationality, or national or ethnic origin.' The term 'ethnic origin' has been held to be wider than 'race'.

In *Mandla v Dowell Lee* (1983), the House of Lords explained that for a group to constitute an ethnic group, it needed certain characteristics, ie

- a long history;
- a common cultural tradition;
- a common geographical origin;
- a common language;

- a common religion;
- a minority group.

  The following have been held to be ethnic groups:

  Sikhs – in *Mandla v Powell Lee* (1983);

  Jews – in *Seide v Gillette Industries* (1980);

  Gypsies – in *CRE v Dutton*.

  The following have been found not to be separate ethnic groups:

  Non-Welsh-speaking Welshmen in *Gwynedd CC v Jones* (1986);

  Rastafarians – in *Crown Suppliers v Dawkins* (1993).

  Muslims do not belong to an ethnic group but it has been held that discrimination against Muslims can be indirect discrimination against Asians.

- Prohibits discrimination 'on the grounds of race, etc'

  (*Cf* SDA which prohibits discrimination on the grounds of 'her' sex.) In *Showboat Entertainment Centre v Owens* (1984) Owens who was white was dismissed from her job as a manager for failing to obey an order to exclude black people. In *Wilson v TB Steelworks* (1979) an offer of a job to a white woman was withdrawn when she revealed that her husband was black. In both of the above cases there was discrimination on the grounds of race.

- Specifically states that segregation is to count as 'less favourable treatment'. But see *Pell v Mogdill* (1980).

Genuine occupational qualifications

These comprise:

- dramatic or other performances;
- artists or photographers models;
- ethnic restaurants;
- personal services.

Disability Discrimination Act 1995

Definition of disability

A person is disabled 'if he has a physical or mental impairment which has a long-term adverse effect on his ability to carry out normal everyday activities'.

The Disability Discrimination Regulations 1996 provide guidance on what amounts to a disability; the following do not qualify: addiction to alcohol or any other drug, unless originally medically prescribed; personality disorders, a tendency to steal, or start fires, or to physical or sexual abuse; exhibitionism or voyeurism; disfiguring tattoos; hay fever.

The definition will however cover:

- persons who have had a disability, but who have now recovered;
- persons who have some means of coping with the disability;
- a progressive condition (eg cancer or multiple sclerosis) from the time it has an adverse effect on a person's day-to-day activities.

Meaning of discrimination

It is unlawful for a person to treat a person less favourably for a reason related to his disability, than he would treat others to whom that reason would not apply.

Unlike direct discrimination on the ground of sex or race, this less favourable treatment can be justified by the employer showing that the disability is 'both material to the circumstances of the particular case, and substantial'. Regulations have confirmed that the discrimination is justified:

- in the case of pay – if it arises from a general scheme of performance related pay;
- in the case of pension benefits – where the cost of those benefits is substantially greater;
- in the case of insurance – if the disability is relevant to the risk insured.

There is no provision covering indirect discrimination but s 6 requires that where any arrangement made by an employer or any physical feature of the premises puts a disabled job applicant or employee at a substantial disadvantage, there is an obligation on the employer to make a reasonable adjustment in order to prevent the disadvantage arising. An unjustified failure to meet this duty amounts to unlawful discrimination.

It is argued that this provision prevents indirect discrimination.

Regulations have identified physical features as covering the design and construction of a building; the approach, the access or the exits; fixtures, fittings, furniture, equipment, or materials.

It is conceded, however, that it is not reasonable for an employer to alter features which are covered by Building Regulations, or a term in a mortgage, or a restrictive covenant, or a lease where consent has to be obtained.

Remedies

Complaints must be presented to a tribunal within three months. The tribunal may make a declaration, order the employer to pay compensation, and/or recommend that the employer take specified action. The damages are to be based on the assessment of damages in the law of tort. There is no upper limit.

The Act came into operation on 2 December 1996 – so far there are few reported cases.

Criticisms of the Act

- Narrow definition of disability, eg does not cover those with a reputation for disability, but with no actual disability.
- The extent to which employers can plead that the discrimination is justified.
- No body has been set up to review and enforce it, *cf* CRE, EOC.
- Act is not applicable to small employers, ie under 20 employees.

Religion

There is no general provision covering discrimination on religious grounds, but it may, in certain circumstances amount to indirect discrimination on racial grounds. The Fair Employment Act 1989 which does deal with religious discrimination applies only to Northern Ireland.

Age

There has been much discussion in recent years concerning age discrimination, and its effects. However, there is as yet no specific legislation covering age discrimination, although it has in certain cases been dealt with under sex discrimination.

Article 2 of the Treaty of Amsterdam will prohibit discrimination on the grounds of age, religious beliefs and sexual orientation.

The influence of EU Law on UK discrimination law

As can be seen from the above, Article 119 and its accompanying directives have had a major influence on sex discrimination and equal pay in the UK. The influence has been exerted in the following ways:

- Enforcement actions taken by the European Commission against the UK government. For example the decision of the ECJ that the EPA 1970 did not meet the requirements of Article 119 as explained in the Equal Pay Directive led to the Equal Pay (Amendment) Regulations 1983 which incorporated the principle of 'equal value' into UK law.

  The decision of the ECJ that the SDA 1975 did not fully meet the requirements of the Equal Treatment Directive led to the Sex Discrimination Act 1986 which withdrew exceptions covering small businesses, private houses and midwives.

- Judicial review

  In *R v Secretary of State for Employment, ex p EOC* (1995), the House of Lords declared that the provisions in the EPCA 1978 whereby part-time employees working for fewer than 16 hours a week were subject to different qualifying requirements for redundancy payments or claims of unfair dismissal were incompatible with the Equal Treatment Directive. This decision led to the Employment Protection (part-time employees) Regulations 1995 which led to the harmonisation of qualifying conditions for full-time and part-time workers.

- The Direct Effect of Article 119, and the direct effect against 'emanations of the state' of the accompanying directives.

  Thus UK claimants can use EC law as free-standing right enforceable by the tribunals or courts. For example:

  (a) To take advantage of the more generous meaning given to 'pay' in Article 119. It has been held to cover, *inter alia*, non-contractual payments such as post-retirement travel concessions (*Garland v British Rail Engineering Ltd* (1982)); ex-gratia and voluntary redundancy payments (*Barber v Guardian Royal Exchange* (1990)); contractual and statutory redundancy payments (*Barber*); sick pay (*Rinner-Kuhn v FWW Spezial Gebaudereingung GmbH* (1989)); paid leave for attending a training course (*Arbeiter wohlfahrt der Stadt Berlin v Botel* (1992)); Occupational Pension Schemes (*Barber*).

(b) To choose a predecessor as a comparator as is allowed under Article 119 (*Macarthys Ltd v Smith* (1981)).

(c) To require an employer to justify a factor which has a disparate effect on the incomes of groups of men and women as in *Enderby v Frenchay AHA* (above) following *Danfoss* (above), in the same way that indirect discrimination has to be justified under the SDA 1975. This allows the tribunals to investigate why occupations made up mainly of women are paid less than predominantly male occupations employed by the same employer. This would not be possible under the EPA 1970, which does not provide for indirect discrimination.

- UK courts have to interpret UK legislation in accordance with EU law either by:

(a) referring a query to the ECJ as in *Webb v EMU Cargo*. At the time of writing answers are awaited from the ECJ on a number of issues, including whether sex discrimination covers sexual orientation; whether compensation for unfair dismissal is 'pay', etc;

(b) itself interpreting the SDA or the EPA in order to comply with EU legislation, as in *Pickstone v Freemans*.

Most of the advances in sex discrimination or equal pay since the mid-1970s have has in fact been made as a result of EU law. And it does not end there; there have also been changes made to the RRA 1996, in order to keep it in tune with the changes made to the SDA 1995, eg the removal of the upper limit on damages: and as can be seen from the above, Article 119 has also led to changes being made to the qualifications for bring a claim for redundancy payments or unfair dismissal.

Criticisms of discrimination law

The growth of anti-discrimination legislation is seen as useful in introducing the principles of equal treatment into employment It is also praised in that it covers all workers, not merely employees, and thus provides an example to other areas of employment law in how to avoid the problems associated with contracts of service and contracts for service.

It is criticised, however, for its uneven operation, eg there is no commission to oversee the law on disability as there is on sex and race, not all forms of discrimination are covered, eg there is no prohibition on discrimination on the grounds of age or religious belief (except in Northern Ireland) or sexual orientation.

However, the proposed Article 3 of the Treaty of Amsterdam seeks to prohibit discrimination on the basis of gender, sexual orientation, race, ethnic origin, religious beliefs, and age and this will ultimately filter into UK law.

Sex discrimination legislation has been criticised on the basis that the legislation takes the male as a norm; women are expected to fit into a structure designed to suit men, eg full time work, rewards for continuous employment or seniority. Most women have fragmented careers, the difference in the career structures should be recognised. Women, it is argued, should not be treated as 'deficit men'.

Both race and sex discrimination legislation are presently about equality of opportunity not equality of outcomes. They are even-handed, applying equally to both men and women, and to all races thus making positive action impossible (except in respect of s 48 of the SDA).

Procedures

- Cases must be brought by individuals – an employee may find difficulty in knowing whether he or she has been discriminated against in the first place; discovery of document is not available until the case has commenced.

   Legal aid is not available: the EOC and the CRE may give assistance but both are short of funds. Class actions are not possible.

- The procedures are complicated – the burden of proof is on the claimant, cf unfair dismissal where it is up to the employer to prove that the dismissal is fair, on the ground that he made the decision and he has all the facts at his command. The position has been improved somewhat by *King v China Co Ltd* (see above). The European Commission is currently considering a directive on the burden of proof.

   Procedures in cases involving sex discrimination are particularly complicated. The EOC has recommended that the SDA and the ECPA should be replaced by a single act. In addition cases may be 'lobbed' back and fore to the ECJ. The case of *Enderby v Frenchay Health Authority* took over 10 years to come to a conclusion.

- It is also alleged that industrial tribunals have difficulty in dealing with discrimination cases. They are comparatively few; specialisation in tribunal staff is not allowed and it has been argued that tribunals often apply quite wrongly the 'reasonableness' test to discrimination cases.

Remedies

- The position with regard to remedies has improved following decisions of the ECJ in *Marshall v SW Hants AHA (No 2)* (1993) (see above p 78) but damages are still not available as of right for indirect race discrimination.
- Recommendations can be made by the court to an employer, but there have been no orders to reinstate or hire which contrasts unfavourably with the position in the US.

5 Termination of the contract of employment – wrongful dismissal

You should be familiar with the following areas:

- the consequences which may follow a termination of employment
- the requirements of an action for wrongful dismissal
- the remedies for wrongful dismissal

Termination of a contract of employment

There are contractual and statutory consequences to a termination of employment:

1 Wrongful dismissal – dismissal in breach of contract; contractual remedy.

2 Unfair dismissal – dismissal contrary to the provisions of the Employment Rights Act 1996; statutory remedy.

3 Redundancy payments – entitlement under the Employment Rights Act 1996; statutory remedy.

Wrongful dismissal (dismissal in breach of contract)

The statutory provisions governing unfair dismissal (see below) were brought in because of the weaknesses in the protection given to employees by the common law, which did not consider the fairness or otherwise of any dismissal but merely looked at whether the correct procedures had been followed and where the damages, in any case, would not exceed the wages due under the appropriate period of notice. However, there has been a revival of interest in recent years in wrongful dismissal particularly in the case of highly paid employees with entitlements to long periods of notice or with fixed term contracts because of deficiencies in the arrangement for the statutory claims, eg:

- low success rates of applications;
- the low level of compensation;
- many employees are not qualified to claim because of the two-year qualification period;
- the industrial tribunals are reluctant to order re instatement or re-engagement.

In addition, the statutory requirements for the length of notice and the disciplinary procedures to be set out in the written particulars have also assisted employees in identifying a breach of contract on the part of the employer.

Grounds for claims of wrongful dismissal

The employer has committed a breach of contract, eg:

- Proper notice has not been given – either Contractual Notice or Reasonable Notice if no contractual period is stated. A minimum period of notice is now also granted by s 86 of the Employment Rights Act 1996.
- Contractual procedures have not been followed, eg the contractual disciplinary procedures.
- The contract may stipulate that dismissal is only possible on certain grounds, eg university tenure.

Defences available to the employer

There was no dismissal

For example where:

- The employee resigned.

  But it must be a genuine resignation, not one given under a threat that if he does not resign, he will be dismissed. In such a case, he will be treated as dismissed. However, in *Staffs CC v Donovan* (1981) it was held that the institution of disciplinary proceedings was not a threat of dismissal.

Constructive resignation was at one time promoted as an argument against dismissal where an employee had committed a fundamental breach of contract – it was argued that he had dismissed himself. However, in *London Transport Executive v Clarke* (1981) where an employee left for an extended holiday in Jamaica contrary to express instructions, it was pointed out by the Court of Appeal that in the law of contract a fundamental breach does not terminate the contract. It allows the other party to terminate the contract if he so wishes. Therefore it was the employer in that case not the employee who had terminated the contract.

(The court in this case accepted that the 'elective' theory, ie that termination of the contract takes place when the innocent party accepts a repudiation of the contract, not when the other party actually repudiates it, applies to contracts of employment as it does to other contracts. This had previously been a matter of dispute.)

• The termination was by mutual agreement.

Again, there must be a genuine agreement, eg the employee left in return for various benefits as in *Birch v University of Liverpool* (1985) where academic staff who volunteered for early retirement were held to have terminated their contracts by agreement or in *Sheffield v Oxford Controls* (1985) where the applicant resigned after being promised £10,000 and certain other benefits.

Note
Problems have arisen with regard to agreements that the contract will automatically come to an end on the happening of a future event. In *Igbo v Johnson Matthey Chemicals* (1985), an employee signed an agreement which stated that if she did not return to work by a stated date, her contract of employment would automatically terminate on that date. The EAT considered that this was an agreed termination, but the Court of Appeal pointed out that it contravened EPCA now s 203 of the ERA 1996 in that it purported to limit the effect of the employment protection legislation, and it was therefore void. Presumably, such a provision will ensure that there is no dismissal for the purpose of a wrongful dismissal claim, but will be ineffective in claims for unfair dismissal or redundancy payments.

• The contract was frustrated.

'Frustration occurs whenever the law recognises that without the fault of either party, a contractual obligation has become incapable of being performed, because the circumstances in which performance is called for would render it a thing different from that which was undertaken in the contract.'

At common law a contract of employment is frustrated by the death of an employer, compulsory liquidation of a company, and the dissolution of a partnership. (But see the ERA 1996 for position on unfair dismissal.)

Two circumstances create particular difficulties with regard to frustration of a contract of employment.

Sickness

The courts have as a general rule been reluctant to hold that a contract has been frustrated because of sickness, because a wide acceptance of the doctrine would undermine the aims of employment protection legislation.

However, in *Egg Stores v Leibovici* (1977) the EAT stated that the following factors should be taken into account:

- the length of previous employment;
- the nature of the job;
- the nature, length and effect of the disability;
- the need for the work to be done by a replacement;
- the risk of acquiring liability to a replacement;
- whether wages had been paid;
- the acts and statements of the employer;
- whether, in all the circumstances, the employer could have been expected to wait longer.

In *Notcutt v Universal Equipment Company Co Ltd* (1986) a 64-year-old employee who had worked for the company for 36 years suffered a heart attack. After a while it became obvious that he would never be able to work again. The Court of Appeal confirmed the approach taken in *Egg Stores v Leibovici* and held that the contract was frustrated.

In *Williams v Watsons Luxury Coaches Ltd* (1990) the Court of Appeal approved of 'Leibovici' but stated that the court must be careful not to use the doctrine too easily.

Imprisonment

The doctrine of frustration does not apply if the frustrating event was self-induced. The courts have accepted, however, in a number of cases that imprisonment can frustrate a contract. In *Shepherd v Jerrom* (1986), the Court of Appeal held that imprisonment was potentially a frustrating event, the offence is the fault of the person who committed it, but the term of imprisonment is the decision of the court. In this the applicant had entered into a four-year apprenticeship agreement, when after 21 months he was sentenced to six months in Borstal. The Court of Appeal held that the contract was frustrated. Imprisonment will not necessarily amount to frustration in all cases, however, eg if the event had been foreseen.

• The contract was completed.

For example the contract was for the completion of a particular task. In *Ryan v Shipboard Maintenance* (1980) it was held there was no dismissal as the contract had been discharged by performance.

• The contract was a fixed term contract.

There is no dismissal at common law, when the fixed term comes to an end, but see unfair dismissal provisions.

The dismissal was justified

• It was in accordance with the contract.
• It followed repudiatory conduct by the employee, eg gross misconduct. The law of contract allows the other party to treat the contract as discharged where there has been a fundamental breach on the part of one party.

Examples of gross misconduct – the employee has gone on strike; worked to rule; has stolen from the employer; has committed an act of violence; sometimes disobedience or drunkenness would qualify. It may be one major incident, or it may be a collection of minor incidents as in *Pepper v Webb* (1969) where a refusal to obey accompanied by swearing was the 'last straw'. Some conduct may also be labelled in the contract as a condition.

Note

A fundamental breach of contract by the employer allows the employee to leave and claim damages for breach of contract, as in *Hanley v Pease* (1915) or in accordance with the 'elective' theory, he may remain and claim damages for breach of contract as in *Rigby v Ferodo Ltd* (see above p 25).

Remedies

Damages

Damages are the normal remedy for breach of contract. They will include:

- normal income plus fringe benefits during period of notice or period of fixed term contract;
- loss of right to claim for unfair dismissal (if applicable).

They will not include compensation for injured feelings, or humiliation, or the fact that future earnings are affected (*Bliss v SE Thames AHA* (1985)). The injured party must mitigate his loss, ie he must try to obtain another post. It was held in *Yetton v Eastwoods Froy* (1966), however, that he need not accept any job, eg one much lower in status and income than his previous job.

Deductions

The following sums will be deducted:

- other earnings;
- tax (on sums above £30,000);
- National Insurance contributions;
- jobseekers allowance and/or income support.

Equitable remedies

Traditionally equitable remedies have not been considered suitable for breaches of contracts of employment. Specific performance is not available. Injunctions, however, have traditionally been available to an employer to enforce a negative covenant in a contract of employment (*Warner Bros v Nelson*).

Since the 'elective theory' has now been accepted as applying to contracts of employment (see *TLE v Clarke* above) this provides employees with a possibility of obtaining an injunction to restrain the employer from committing a breach of contract, eg by dismissing the employee without the proper formalities.

Interlocutory injunctions have been issued to prevent an employer from proceeding with a dismissal in the following cases:

- Where trust and confidence still remains. In *Hill v Parsons* (1972) the Court of Appeal issued an injunction where an employer had been reluctantly forced to dismiss a long-serving employee in a closed shop, on the ground that both employer and employee still had confidence in each other. It has been argued that where the case is brought to obtain the salary whilst the proper procedures are followed, then the preservation of trust and confidence is immaterial.

- To prevent an employer from committing a breach of contract, eg by ignoring a contractual dismissal procedure. In *Jones v Lee* (1980) the court restrained a local authority from dismissing a headmaster until it had granted him a contractual right to a hearing. In *Irani v Hants Area Health Authority* (1985) and *Powell v Brent* (1987) the fact that trust and confidence remained between the parties was again considered important. However, in *Wadstock v Brent* (1990) and *Robb v Hammersmith and Fulham* (1991) the preservation of trust and confidence between the parties was ignored.

- Where the contract allows dismissal only on specific grounds.

In *McLelland v Northern Ireland GHSB* (1957) the court maintained that the employer could be restrained by an injunction or a declaration in such cases.

It has been suggested that a dismissed employee with suitable grounds should immediately seek an injunction, otherwise he may have been deemed to have accepted the termination.

Declarations

Declarations were issued by the court in *Gunton v Richmond* upon Thames (1980) to declare that the contract still existed and also in *McLelland v N Ireland*.

Public law remedies

Certain public law remedies may be available to certain office holders through judicial review.

Despite the returning interest in wrongful dismissal, unfair dismissal, ie dismissal contrary to the ERA 1996 is still the most suitable remedy for most employees.

6 Termination of the contract of employment – unfair dismissal

> You should be familiar with the following areas:
>
> - the qualifications necessary to bring an action of unfair dismissal
> - the 'potentially fair' grounds for dismissal
> - the tests for 'reasonableness in the circumstances'

Unfair dismissal

Deakin and Morris state that the law relating to unfair dismissal and redundancy payments affects the entire structure of the employment relationship.

- It sets the norms for lesser disciplinary sanctions, eg suspension or demotion.
- It qualifies the common law right to insist on unilateral change.
- Dismissal law is the bulwark of those fundamental employment rights currently recognised by UK law, eg trade union membership, health and safety protection, pregnancy and maternity rights.

Aims of dismissal legislation

The following have been suggested as the main aims of dismissal legislation.

- To provide job security; not by giving absolute protection, but protection against arbitrary managerial decision-making.
- To provide a property right in a job. This however has been disputed as employment protection has very little resemblance to actual property rights. There are few 'jobs for life' today.

Hugh Collins states that the purpose is to provide a right to dignity and autonomy for the employee. Employees must be treated with respect for their person and individuality, but dismissals which are for rational considerations (redundancy or incapacity) and are carried out with due process and procedural fairness are legitimate.

- To increase managerial efficiency. It was felt that introducing formal disciplinary and dismissal procedures would enable employers to manage their workforce more efficiently and improve personnel management generally, which pre-1971 was very poor in many organisations.

- To improve industrial relations. It was believed that the improvement in personnel management, and the fact there would be an impartial forum to decide the fairness of a dismissal would improve industrial relations and in particular would lessen the industrial conflict which often followed dismissals.

- To improve labour market flexibility. One of the main aims of the Redundancy Payments Act 1966 was to give employees displaced from declining industries incentives to abandon resistance to technical change, and enhance job mobility.

The Employment Rights Act 1996 provides that, subject to certain exceptions, every employee has the right not to be unfairly dismissed.

Note

- A complaint of unfair dismissal does not depend on whether there has been a breach of contract, but on whether the dismissal is unfair according to statutory criteria.

- The concept of unfair dismissal goes beyond the contractual position in that it provides employees with a measure of job protection. It met the requirements of the ILO recommendations which were accepted by the UK in 1964, and it also corresponded with similar developments in other countries.

Burden of evidence and proof before tribunals

Stage 1 – The burden of proof is on the applicant to show:

- he or she was an employee;
- he or she was not excluded from bringing an action;
- he or she brought the claim within the time limits;
- he or she was dismissed.

Stage 2 – The burden of proof is on the employer to show that he had a valid reason for the dismissal.

Stage 3 –

- The tribunal must be satisfied that the employer acted 'reasonably in the circumstances'.
- The tribunal must consider all the facts and circumstances and decide whether or not the dismissal was fair.

They must take into account the size and administrative resources of the employers undertaking, and the question shall be determined 'in accordance with equity and the merits of the case'.

Stage 1

These requirements also apply to a claim for redundancy payments.

It is essential that the student refers back to certain sections of Chapters 2 and 3 where this is indicated in the text, as these are essential features of the right to bring a claim

The applicant must show that:

A – He is an employee

- see Chapter 2 for the difference between contracts of employment and contracts for self-employment; and
- the effect of contractual flaws on the contract of employment, eg illegality.

B – He is not excluded from bringing the action

1 He has been 'continually employed' for less than two years.
- For meaning of 'continuous employment' see Chapter 3, pp 36–43;
- The two-year qualifying period.

This was challenged in *R v Secretary of State for Employment, ex p Seymour Smith* (1995) on the ground that it indirectly discriminated against women. The Court of Appeal held that there were considerable differences between the proportion of men and women who could comply with the two-year rule between 1985 and 1991 and that the government could not justify the rule. They declined to quash the rule, however, pending an appeal to the House of Lords. The case, however, has no necessary relevance for dismissals in 1997 as the statistical evidence relates only to the period 1985–91. The matter has now been referred to the ECJ for a ruling.

Four questions should be asked in order to establish two years' continuous employment:

(a) When did the employee start work?

This has been held to be the starting date on the contract of employment rather than the actual day on which he started (*Salvation Army v Dewsbury* (see Chapter 3, p 40).

(b) When was the effective date of termination?

- When the contract was terminated by notice – the date on which the notice expired.

- When the contract was terminated without notice, the date on which the employer told the employee he was fired.

In the above cases, the statutory period of notice can be added to the date if it is not given, unless the dismissal is justified on ground of gross misconduct. The correct contractual period will not be added but it was suggested in *TBA Industrial Products v Moorland* (1982) that if an employee loses his statutory rights because of instant dismissal, he could bring an action for wrongful dismissal, claiming loss of statutory rights as one head of damages.

- Where a fixed term contract is not renewed – the date on which it expired.

- Constructive dismissal – if the employee leaves without notice, the date of departure; if he gives notice, the expiry of the notice.

- Dismissal with pay in lieu of notice.

The date of termination will depend on an interpretation of the dismissal letter. In *Dedman v British Building & Engineering Appliances Ltd* (1974) the employee was handed a letter on 5 May which said 'there is no alternative but to dismiss you immediately'. He left that day, but received his full pay for May together with another months pay 'in lieu of notice'. Held: the contract was terminated on 5 May.

However, if he is given 'paid leave', then the effective date of termination will be the date on which his notice expired.

In *Adams v Sankey Ltd* (1980) a dismissal letter stated: 'You are given 12 weeks' notice from 5 November. You will not be expected to work out your notice, but will receive money in lieu of notice.' Held: the effective date of termination was 12 weeks from 5 November.

- Where there is an internal appeals procedure.

  The date of termination will be the date of the original dismissal unless the contract specifically states that the employee is not dismissed until the appeal is heard, eg a suspension without pay until the appeal is heard does not preserve the contract until after the appeal.

(c) Is the difference between the two dates two years? – ie two calendar years.

(d) Was the employment continuous? – see Chapter 3, pp 36–43.

2 He is over the normal retiring age on the effective date of termination.

The normal retiring age will be the age at which employees expect to retire.

- This will normally be the contractual retiring age, but this can be rebutted by evidence that the contractual age has been abandoned in practice.

  In *Waite v GCHQ* (1983) it was held that the normal retiring age was the age at which the employees can normally expect to be compelled to retire.

- A normal retiring age established by practice can be varied by the employers announcement, as this will change the expectation of the employees *Hughes v Dept of Health & Social Security* (1985). But it has been confirmed by the EAT that the normal retiring age cannot be reduced below the contractual retiring age unless the contract has been lawfully varied (*Bratko v Beloit Walmsley Ltd* (1995)).

- Different groups of employees can have different retiring ages (*Coy v DHSS* (1985)).

- If there is no normal retiring age, then the retiring age will be 65. In *Barclays Bank v O'Brian* (1994) the employer stated that the normal retiring age was 60, but allowed one group to stay on. When the applicants were dismissed at 60, they claimed that there was no normal retiring age and therefore 65 should apply. The EAT disagreed – where the employer had laid down a normal age, that applied even if there were exceptions.

- 65 is the maximum retiring age for redundancy payments.

- Unfair dismissal claimants whose dismissal was union related may however have a higher normal retiring age.

3   He normally works outside Great Britain.

The Court of Appeal have stated that this is to be ascertained by consulting the contract of employment.

Thus in *Hillier v Martintrux* (1978) an HGV driver who spent 90% of his time on the continent was not excluded. His work was controlled in the UK; he was paid in sterling and was subject to UK income tax. In *Janata Bank v Ahmed* (1981), on the other hand, an employee of a Bangladeshi Bank was held to work ordinarily outside the UK on the basis that his appointment here was in the nature of a posting and he could be recalled at any time.

4   He is an employee under a fixed term contract of one year or more who has agreed in writing to renounce his unfair dismissal rights. (In other cases, the unfair dismissal provisions cannot be excluded by agreement, s 140 declares that any provision in an agreement is void in so far as it purports to exclude or limit the operation of the unfair dismissal provisions.)

5   He belongs to a miscellaneous category, eg share fishermen; the police; members of the armed forces and other crown employees where the minister has issued an exempting certificate.

C – He has brought the claim within the time limit

A claim is commenced when it is delivered to the Central Office of industrial tribunals. An action for unfair dismissal must be commenced:

- Within three months of the effective date of termination (see above p 108 for date of termination).

- Within such further period as the industrial tribunal considers reasonable in cases where it is satisfied that it was not 'reasonably practical' for the complaint to be presented within the three month period. It was held in *Palmer v Southend BC* (1984) that this is a question of fact and not law and will rarely be subject to appeal. Ignorance of ones rights will not normally be sufficient nor will awaiting the results of an internal appeal (*Palmer v Southend BC*) or criminal proceedings. Not learning of a material fact until after the time limit will be 'just cause'.

- It has been stated that tribunals should be fairly strict in enforcing the time limits.

- If the applicant is wrongly advised by a 'skilled adviser', ie solicitor, trade union official, CAB adviser, then his action should be against the advisor (*London International College v Sen*

(1993)) but not where the wrong information was given by an employee of the industrial tribunal.

D – He has been dismissed

A dismissal takes place in the following circumstances.

(i) Termination by the employer with or without notice.

In most cases this is straightforward, but problems can arise, eg:

- in the case of words of abuse, eg 'f— off'. In *Stern v Simpson* (1983) it was stated that it is not the actual words used which are important but the intention behind them, which must be ascertained from the surrounding circumstances; or words used in the heat of the moment (*Martin v Yeoman Aggregates* (1983)).
- There must be an actual dismissal not just a warning of dismissal in the future.
- Resignations or mutually-agreed terminations do not amount to a dismissal, nor is there a dismissal when the contract is frustrated (see Wrongful dismissal – Chapter 5, pp 98–100).

(ii) Expiry of a fixed term contract without renewal

If however the contract is to last for at least a year, then an employee may agree in writing to waive the unfair dismissal provisions. It was held by the Court of Appeal in *Dixon v BBC* (1979) that a contract for a fixed term 'unless previously determined by one week's notice' was nevertheless a fixed term contract. It is important to distinguish, however, between a contract for a fixed term and a contract for a particular purpose. In *Brown v Knowsley* (1986) temporary teachers had been engaged for 'as long as funds are provided by the MSC'. It was held that this was a contract for a particular purpose, and automatically terminated when the purpose was achieved.

(iii) Constructive dismissal

The employee terminates his contract in circumstances entitling him to terminate it without notice by reason of the employers conduct.

The Court of Appeal has held that to entitle the employee to resign, the employers conduct must amount to a breach of contract. In *Western Excavating Ltd v Sharp* (1978), an employee was suspended for five days without pay. Being penniless, he asked his employer for a loan. This was refused. He claimed unfair dismissal on the grounds that he had been forced to resign because of his employers unreasonable conduct. His claim was upheld by the industrial tribunal and by the EAT. The Court of Appeal, however, held that 'unreasonable conduct' was not the test; there had to be a breach of contract. In this case there was no contractual obligation to make the payment, and therefore no breach of contract, and therefore no dismissal.

It is only, therefore, in those cases where there has been a significant breach of contract can there be a constructive dismissal. The contractual rules with regard to a fundamental breach are followed.

Examples of breaches by the employer.

- Attempting to impose a unilateral change in the terms of employment, eg demotion, change in the nature of the work, change in location of employment.
- Doing something not authorised by the contract of employment, eg suspension without pay.
- Breach of an implied term in the contract.

In *BAC v Austin* (1978) a failure to investigate a complaint about the inadequacy of protective equipment was held to be a breach of the implied duty to take reasonable care for the health and safety of employees.

The development of the implied term of mutual trust and confidence has greatly expanded the range of constructive dismissal, and it has been argued that it has to a large degree outflanked the purely contractual approach laid down in *Western Excavating* (see Implied terms, Chapter 2, p 31).

It has been extended to cover, *inter alia*:

- false accusations of dishonesty and theft (*Robinson v Crompton Parkinson* (1978));
- using foul and abusive language (*Palmanor Ltd v Cedron* (1978));
- making unjustified complaints and warnings (*Walker v Josiah Wedgwood* (1978));
- sexual harassment (*Gardener v Beresford* (1978));
- dressing down an employee in front of colleagues (*Hilton International Ltd v Protopapa* (1990));
- assault (*Bracebridge Engineering v Darby* (1990)).

(Note also *United Bank v Akhtar and White v Reflecting Roadstuds*, which deal with the question of whether this implied term can be used in conjunction with an express term. See Chapter 2, p 26.)

Note

• Lawful conduct by the employer cannot amount to a constructive dismissal.

• If there is a genuine dispute as to the contractual position, there is no repudiation by the employer.

• A repudiation may be anticipatory, eg the employer announces that he is going to implement unilateral changes in the terms and conditions in the future.

• If the employer has committed a repudiatory breach and the employee does not take any action, then there is a danger that this will be construed as an agreement by the employee to a variation of the contract.

A constructive dismissal is not automatically a fair dismissal. See, Variation of contract, Chapter 3, pp 25, 26.

Stage 2

The reason for the dismissal

The onus is on the employer to establish the reason for the dismissal, ie 'the set of facts known to the employer or beliefs held by him which caused him to dismiss the employee' (*Devis & Sons v Atkins*, see below). Section 92 of the ERA 1996 provides that an employee with two years service who has been dismissed (apart from those constructively dismissed) may require the employer to provide a written reason for the dismissal. If the employer unreasonably fails to do so within 14 days, then the employee may complain to an industrial tribunal which may order payment of two weeks' salary to the employee.

The employer must be consistent. The reason for the dismissal should not differ from that on the 'written reasons for the dismissal' or the 'Notice of Appearance'. An employer may not plead in the tribunal a reason which he has not stated in the Notice of Appearance, unless the facts he has related are capable of satisfying a different label. For instance the employer may have quoted facts to establish a 'redundancy', but those fact actually disclose a reorganisation of the business which comes under the heading of 'some other substantial reason'.

The reasons must be known to the employer at the time the dismissal took place. He cannot rely on after discovered facts to justify the dismissal. In *Devis & Sons v Atkins* (1977) an employee was dismissed for disobeying instructions. Evidence of dishonesty was later discovered. The House of Lords held that this could not be relied upon by the employer as the fairness of the dismissal was based on the reasonability of the employers conduct and this had to be judged on facts known to him at the time he took the decision.

After discovered conduct may, however, be relevant:

- in assessing the amount of the compensation (see below);
- in relation to an appeal hearing by the employer.

If the appeal is turned down then the dismissal dates from the original decision to dismiss. It was held by the House of Lords in *West Midland Cooperative Society v Tipton* (1986) that the appeal is part of the dismissal process and any information favourable to the employee must be taken into account. They also approved the statement in *National Heart and Chest Hospitals v Nambiar* (1981) that new misconduct revealed during an appeal could not be used by the employer to justify the dismissal under consideration, but could provide grounds for a subsequent dismissal.

Potentially fair reasons for dismissal

(a) Capability or qualification

This covers:

- Competence

    An employer must prove the inability or incompetence of the employee. General allegations without proof are not normally enough. A pattern of incompetence is generally required, but a single incident if sufficiently serious can suffice. In *Alidair v Taylor* (1978) a pilot was dismissed after he had landed a plane in a dangerous manner. The subsequent dismissal was held to be fair as the employer had clearly lost all confidence in the capability of the pilot.

    Formal warnings are normally a matter for misconduct not inability. However, it was pointed out by the EAT in *James v Waltham Holy Cross UDC* (1973) that: 'An employer should be very slow to dismiss upon terms that an employee is incapable of performing his work without first telling him of the respects in which he is failing to do his job adequately, warning him of the possibility or likelihood of dismissal on this ground, and giving him an opportunity to improve his performance.' Dismissal without warning would be justified, however, if it is shown that the employee is irredeemably incompetent.

The employee should also show that he has investigated the reason for the incompetence, eg has the employee been properly trained? In *Davison v Kent* (1975), the applicant was dismissed for assembling nearly 500 components in the wrong sequence. She claimed she had worked to the chargehand's instructions. The chargehand denied having given her any instructions. Held: the dismissal was fair.

Other matters to be established: Has he been properly supervised? Did he have proper equipment? Had he been given an adequate job description? Did he have appropriate conditions of work?

- Neglectful incompetence

  The employee is capable of doing the work but is neglecting to do so. In this case the employer is dealing with misconduct and should invoke the disciplinary procedure.

- Ill-health

  In the case of long-term ill-health, the tribunal will have to balance the needs of the business and the welfare of the employee.

  Matters taken into account are similar to those taken into account in the case of frustration. See *Egg Stores v Leibovici* (1977); Chapter 5, p 100.

  In *East Lindsay v Daubenay* (1977) the employer's own physician asked a doctor to examine the employee, and as a result of his advice recommended retirement. The decision was considered unfair as the employee had not had an opportunity to see the report, or to discuss it with the employer or to obtain his own medical report. The EAT stressed the importance of consultation. It also stated that the tribunal should consider whether it was reasonable to ask the employer to wait any longer before dismissing in the light of the nature of the employees illness, the actual and potential length of his absence, the circumstances of the individual employee, the urgency for a replacement, and the size and nature of the employers undertaking. The main procedural requirements are concerned with ascertaining the true position, and involve:

  (i) consultation with the employee – this is also useful in acquainting the employee with the employers thinking.

(ii) obtaining up-to-date medical information.

This however can be difficult in view of the Access to Medical Reports Act 1988 and the decision in *Bliss v SE Thames RHA* (1987) which established that the employer does not have the right to insist that the employee undergo a medical examination.

A refusal by the employee however may lead to a finding of a fair dismissal.

(iii) an alternative job, if available and suitable should be offered to the employee

In the case of short-term illnesses (uncertified or certified) warnings may be relevant. In *International Sport Ltd v Thompson* (1980) the applicant was away from work about 25% of the time with various complaints (all covered by a medical certificate) including dizzy spells, anxiety, and nerves, bronchitis, virus infection, cystitis, arthritis of the left knee, dyspepsia and flatulence. She was given a series of warnings including a final warning. The company's medical advisor saw no point in examining her. She was dismissed and the dismissal was held to be fair.

- Qualifications

These must relate to the actual work carried out by the employee.

(b) Conduct

Misconduct is the commonest ground put forward to justify the dismissals.

This ground is not defined in ERA 1996, but a wide range of misconduct has been held by the tribunals to justify dismissal, eg fighting, swearing, drunkenness, neglect, obstructive conduct, absenteeism, insubordination, breach of confidence, sleeping on duty, lateness, horseplay, theft, dangerous conduct, immorality, disloyalty, drug taking, unsuitable clothes, breaking hygiene rules. Disobedience will be a ground for dismissal providing the order was reasonable, and was authorised by the contract. An example of the employers managerial prerogative is seen in *Boychuck v HJ Symonds Holdings Ltd* (1977) where the applicant was held to be fairly dismissed because of her insistence on wearing badges proclaiming her lesbianism. The EAT considered the a reasonable employer can be allowed to decide what, on reflection or mature consideration, can be offensive to customers or fellow employees.

In order to justify the dismissal, however, the misconduct must be serious, or repeated on more than one occasion. Acts of misconduct can be classified into:

- Acts of a trivial nature which will only amount to grounds for dismissal if they are repeated more than once, eg lateness, absenteeism. These will have to be monitored over a period of time and must be dealt with by warnings (informal, then formal).

- Serious matters which may be handled by an immediate final warning.

- Extremely serious matters – gross misconduct – which can lead to instant dismissal. It is helpful if the categories of gross misconduct are spelt out in the disciplinary rules so that all employees will know the consequences of these acts. The employers categorisation of gross misconduct must still be reasonable.

The misconduct must normally be misconduct at work, but misconduct outside work may justify a dismissal if it has a bearing on the employees position at work. In *Richardson v Bradford* (1975) a senior meat inspector employed by the council was convicted of theft from his rugby club. It was held that his subsequent dismissal was fair as the integrity of a public official in a position of trust was of prime importance.

Procedures

In judging misconduct courts and tribunals must have regard to the ACAS Code of Practice No 1 – 'Disciplinary Practices and Procedures in Employment'. Failure to follow the provisions of the Code will not necessarily mean that the dismissal is unfair, but it is strong evidence that it is so.

The Code's recommendations include:

- Disciplinary rules should be clearly stated, preferably in writing, and given to each employee. (There is an exception for firms with under 20 employees.)

- All employers should establish procedures, indicating range of possible sanctions, and who may impose them.

- The procedures must provide for a full investigation of all allegations.

It is not necessary for the employer to prove that the employee was guilty of the alleged offence, but he must show that he had reasonable grounds for that belief.

In *BHS v Burchell* (1980), it was held that the employer must establish:

(a) he genuinely believed that the employee was guilty of the misconduct in question;

(b) he had reasonable grounds for the belief;

(c) he had carried out such investigations as were reasonable in the circumstances.

Problems may arise if the police are investigating an offence. In that case it may be wise for an employer to suspend an employee. on full pay until the hearing. If, however, he is satisfied that the employee is guilty he may dismiss him as in *BHS v Burchell*.

Blanket dismissals are not normally acceptable, but if suspicion falls on more than one person and there is no way of identifying which of them is guilty, then both may be fairly dismissed (*Monie v Coral Racing* (1980); *Parr v Whitbread* (1990)).

• Employees should have adequate notice of any charges, and must be given an opportunity to put their side of the story. They should have a right to be represented by a trade union official, or by a fellow employee at any meeting or hearing. They should be given reasons for the employers decision.

• There should be a right of appeal against the decision.

• Except for gross misconduct, no-one should be dismissed for the first breach of discipline. A four-stage procedure is suggested; oral warning; first written warning; final written warning; disciplinary action; this could be dismissal, or it could be suspension without pay if this is authorised in the contract of employment. This is a suggested procedure; it does not have to be slavishly followed. Warnings should always set out clearly the consequences of further offences.

Problems have arisen with regard to whether warnings for different offences should be treated separately, or whether they should be viewed as part of a general pattern In *Auguste Noel v Curtis* (1990) the applicant was dismissed for the 'abuse of two cheeses'. He had previously received warnings following an altercation with another employee, and for not keeping worksheets. The EAT held that the dismissal was fair as the employer was entitled to look at the overall picture to decide whether the employees behaviour was satisfactory.

No warnings are necessary in the case of gross misconduct, but the other requirements will still apply, eg full investigation, hearings, consistency, appeals. Certain behaviour is generally regarded as gross misconduct, eg violence, dishonesty, but other offences can be treated as gross misconduct by being categorised as such in the disciplinary procedures, eg working for a competitor, clocking offences, but a tribunal may still find the dismissal unfair if the punishment bears no relation to the offence (*Ladbroke Racing v Arnott* (1983)).

- Rules must be applied consistently. Regular waiver of a rule may lead employees into a false state of security. However, in *Haddiannou v Coral Casinos* (1981) the EAT ruled that previous behaviour on the part of the employer was relevant only in three circumstances: (a) to show that some kind of misconduct could be overlooked; (b) to show that the purported reason for the dismissal was not the real one; and (c) to show that some lesser penalty may be more appropriate.

An employees past record should be taken into account. Long service, together with a good record, should normally amount to extenuating circumstances (*Johnson Matthey Metals v Harding* (1978)).

In *P v Nottingham CC* (1992) it was suggested by the Court of Appeal that the fairness of the dismissal may be determined by whether or not the employer has sought alternative employment for the employee. This had previously been relevant only in cases involving redundancy or ill-health.

(c) Redundancy

Redundancy is defined in s 139 of the ERA 1996 – see Chapter 8 pp 144–45.

An employer does not have to justify a redundancy unless it is an obvious sham. A selection for redundancy will automatically be unfair if the employee was selected:

- for a reason connected with trade union membership;
- because of pregnancy or childbirth;
- because the employee had raised certain health and safety issues;
- because the employee had asserted a statutory right.

Automatic unfairness on the ground of contravention of an agreed procedure has now been repealed by the Deregulation and Contracting Out Act 1994.

It was stated in *Bessenden Properties v Corness* (1977) that in all other cases, the employer must carry out the redundancy in a reasonable manner. Certain criteria were suggested and these were confirmed in *Williams v Compair Maxam* (1982) where it was laid down by the EAT, that a tribunal should consider whether:

- Objective criteria were used in the selection of employees for redundancy. It is accepted that the choice of criteria for selection is a matter for management, but management should have objective standards, and there should be some mechanism for ensuring that the criteria were objectively applied.

- The possibility of transfer to other work was investigated (*Vokes v Bear* (1974); *BUSM v Clarke* (1977)).

- Employees were warned and consulted. In *Polkey v Dayton Services Ltd* (below), the House of Lords held that 'in the case of a redundancy, the employer will not act reasonably unless he warns and consults any employees affected or their representatives'. In that case three drivers had been dismissed without warning.

  But see *Duffy v Yeomans & Partners* (below).

- The Trade Union was consulted. See Chapter 10.

  It was held in *Clarke v Eley-Kynoch Ltd* (1983) that a woman who is prejudiced on the ground of sex by a selection procedure for redundancy may complain of indirect discrimination under the SDA 1975.

(d) Continued employment would be a contravention of the law
For example if a driver loses his licence.

A mistaken belief by the employer that he cannot lawfully continue to employ cannot come under this heading, but may qualify as 'some other substantial reason' (*Sandhu v DES* (1978)).

Even in this case, dismissal is not automatically fair. In *Sutcliff & Eaton Ltd v Pinney* (1977) the applicant, a hearing aid dispenser was sacked when he failed to pass the Hearing Aid Council's examination, and was thus removed from the appropriate register of dispensers. Since, however, it was possible for him to obtain an extension of time to take the examination and prosecution was unlikely, his automatic dismissal was considered unfair.

(e) Some other substantial reason (SOSR)
This ground has been much criticised. Its vagueness means that almost any reason will qualify provided it is 'substantial' which again may lie only in the eye of the beholder.

Examples

* Reorganisation of the business

This can be used where the requirements of a redundancy can-not be met. It allows the employer to avoid redundancy pay-ments and unfair dismissal compensation. The tests applied are not very demanding, and seem to have eased over the years.

Thus in *Ellis v Brighton Co-op* (1976) it was stated that the test was whether, if the changes were not implemented, 'the whole business would come to a standstill'.

However, in *Hollister v NFU* (1978) all that was required was a 'good business reason'. And in *Banerjee v City & East London AHA* (1979) a 'discernible advantage to the organisation'.

The EAT and the Court of Appeal would seem to accept that to compete in a free market, employers need the freedom to trim and make efficient their workforce without hindrance. But more recently, however, there are some indications that tribunals will require more information about the need for the reorganisation, eg in *Ladbroke Courage Holidays v Asten* (1981) the EAT indicated that an employer had to produce some evidence of the reorgan-isation as well as the need for it. And in *Humphreys & Glasgow Ltd v Broom & Holt* (1989) the EAT upheld a finding of unfair dis-missal when an employer had increased working hours without any compensation on the ground that he needed to cut over-heads. without showing any evidence for the need.

However it has been argued that these are merely minimal pro-tections for the employee and do not interfere with management prerogative.

* Change in contract terms

Unfair dismissal provisions have proved no defence against unilateral changes in contractual terms or pay. In *RS Components v Urwin* (1973) employees were dismissed when they refused to accept a new clause in their contract restricting them from com-peting with their employer after they left the firm. Held: the dismissal was fair for SOSR. The employer needed this protec-tion in view of the actions of some previous employees.

In *St John of God v Brook* (1992) a charity-run hospital was faced with possible closure for financial reasons. It offered new con-tracts of employment on inferior terms to the workforce. Thirty of the 170 employees refused to accept and were dismissed. The tribunal found the dismissal unfair but the EAT reversed the decision, stating that the test was whether the employer had behaved reasonably in offering the new contracts, not whether it was reasonable for the employees to reject them.

- Temporary work

  SOSR has been used to justify dismissal of temporary workers. In *N Yorkshire v Fay* (1985) the dismissal of a teacher on a fixed term contract was held to be fair as the teacher knew that the post was temporary.

- Employee's private life

  In *Saunders v Scottish National Camps Assoc* (1981) a maintenance handyman at a children's camp was held to have been fairly dismissed for SOSR because many employers would consider it undesirable for homosexuals to be employed in proximity to children.

- Omissions

  In *O'Brian v Prudential* (1979) the claimant was held to have been fairly dismissed for SOSR when he had failed to disclose at a recruitment interview that he had in the past received treatment for a mental disorder.

- Pressure by a customer or a third party

  See *Dobie v Burns International Security* (1984) where the dismissal of an employee by a security firm after Liverpool Airport Authority had refused to accept him as a guard was held fair despite the fact that it would not have been fair if it was based only on the decision of the employer.

- Non-renewal of a fixed term contract

  In *Terry v E Sussex CC* (1976) it was held that non-renewal of a fixed term contract was capable of being for 'some other substantial reason'. The onus will be on the employer to show the reason for the non-renewal and that it was substantial and that the employer had acted reasonably in the circumstances.

- Dismissal for a an economic, technical, or organisational reason entailing changes in the workforce under The Transfer of Undertakings Regulations 1981. See Chapter 7, pp 131, 132.

Stage 3

If the employer establishes a fair reason for the dismissal, then it is for the tribunal to find on the basis of the evidence presented whether or not the employer acted reasonably in treating that ground as a ground for dismissal. The decision must be reasonable in the circumstances and in accordance with equity and the substantial merits of the case.

Note

- The burden of proof in Stage 3 is neutral.
- The tribunal, in assessing the reasonableness of the dismissal, should take into consideration the size and administrative resources of the employers undertaking.
- It involves both substantive and procedural circumstances.

Substantive fairness

1   It is not for the tribunal to substitute its own decision for that of the employer. They should not hold the dismissal unfair because it is not what they would have done in the circumstances. The test is whether the dismissal fell within the range of responses to the employees conduct within which one employer might take one view, and another employer another view.

It has been suggested that the industrial tribunal acts as an 'industrial jury' applying the accepted standards of industry.

In *Iceland Frozen Foods v Jones* (1982) the EAT laid down the following general principles:

- In applying this rule the tribunal must consider the reasonableness of the employers decision, not whether they considered the dismissal fair.
- In judging the reasonableness of the employers conduct, a tribunal must not substitute its own decision as to what was the right course for that of the employer.
- In many cases, there is a band of reasonable responses to the employee's conduct with which one employer may take one view and another quite reasonably take another.
- The function of the tribunal is to determine whether, in the particular circumstances of the case, the decision to dismiss fell within the band of reasonable responses which a reasonable employer might have adopted. If the dismissal falls within the band, then the dismissal is fair. If it falls outside the band, then it is unfair.

2   The employer must have acted reasonably in forming his view of the facts.

See *BHS v Burchell* (1979), p 118.

3   The reasonableness of the employers decision must be judged on the basis of facts known to him at the time of the dismissal.

See *Devis & Sons v Atkins* (1977), p 114.

4   It is the reasonableness of the employers decision which is examined not fairness to the employee. See *Monie v Coral Racing* (1980); *Parr v Whitbread* (1990); *St John of God Ltd v Brooks* (1992), pp 118, 121.

Procedural fairness

The dismissal must also have been carried out in a reasonable manner. The concept of procedural fairness was not contained in the legislation, but has been developed by the courts and tribunals who have been influenced by the ACAS Code of Practice on Disciplinary Procedures and also by the principles of natural justice. The Code's guidelines do not carry the force of law, but any provision which appear to a court or tribunal to be relevant must be taken into account.

The disciplinary procedures to be followed will in most cases be incorporated into the contract of employment.

Thus in the case of:

• Misconduct – the employer should have followed the Code of Practice in respect of warnings, careful investigation of the circumstances, allowing the employee to state his case, and a right of appeal.

• Capability – investigation, consultation, and an offer of alternative work if available. Also a warning when appropriate.

• Redundancy – consultation, a fair selection for redundancy, and an offer of alternative employment when available.

• Other substantial reason – consultation and any other suitable procedure.

The test is whether the employer had acted reasonably, not whether there had been any injustice to the employee.

Previously the Court of Appeal had declared in *British Labour Pump Co Ltd v Byrne* (1979) that, if on the balance of probabilities, dismissal would have followed even if the correct procedures had been adopted, then the dismissal was fair (the 'no difference' rule).

However, this decision was overturned by the House of Lords in *Polkey v Dayton Services Ltd* (1987) where a company had decided to replace four van drivers by two salesmen and a representative. Only one of the drivers was considered suitable for transfer to the new duties, and accordingly the other three were made redundant. The first

Mr Polkey knew of the situation was when he was called into the branch managers office and told he was being made redundant. He was immediately driven home by one of the other drivers, who was then dismissed in the same way on his return. The industrial tribunal found that the company had deliberately disregarded the provisions of the Code of Practice. Having expressed their disapproval of the manner of the dismissal, they nevertheless considered themselves bound by the decision in *British Labour Pump Co Ltd* and held the result would have been the same even if there had been consultation, and that consequently Mr Polkey's dismissal was fair. The EAT and the Court of Appeal considered themselves similarly bound, but the House of Lords held that the rule in *British Pump Co Ltd* was mistaken. In considering whether the employer acted reasonably or un-reasonably – it is what the employer did that must be judged, not what he might have done. Would a reasonable employer have dismissed without consultation or warning as provided in the Code of Practice.

Since *Polkey* the adoption of a correct procedure has been of prime importance in adjudging the fairness of a dismissal. However, even if a dismissal is found to be procedurally unfair it may be possible for the award of compensation (see below) to be reduced on the ground that it would not have made any difference to the ultimate decision. In any case it is now argued that the rule in *Polkey* has been diluted by the decision in *Duffy v Yeomans* (1994) where the Court of Appeal held that in order to comply with *Polkey* an employer who does not consult does not need to take a conscious decision not to consult with an employee. It is sufficient that, judged objectively, the employer does what a reasonable employer might do. It has been pointed out that this decision resembles closely the 'no difference rule' which *Polkey* replaced.

(Query – can *Yeomans* be applied to procedural requirements other than those for redundancy?)

The rules of natural justice
The principles of natural justice, ie the right to be heard and the absence of bias have been considered in connection with:

- The right to state his case

  It was established in *Khanum v Mid Glamorgan AHA* (1978) that the employee should:

  (a) know of the accusations he has to meet;

  (b) be given an opportunity to state his case; and

  (c) the person taking the decision should act in good faith.

- The right of appeal

  This should be set down in the contract of employment. A full judicial style hearing is not necessary but the appeal should not be heard by the same people who took the decision to dismiss. The employee should be informed of his right to appeal, and his right to be represented.

Review by the EAT and the Appeal Court

An appeal lies to EAT only on questions of law, and a decision on whether a dismissal is fair or unfair has been categorised as a question of fact. The Court of Appeal held in *Neale v Hereford & Worcester* (1986) that an industrial tribunal decision can only be attacked if:

- there was a misdirection of law;
- the decision was perverse.

The Court of Appeal has also disapproved of legal guidelines being laid down by the EAT. In *Bailey v BP Oil (Kent Refinery) Ltd* (1980) it was stated that each case must be judged on its facts: 'In our judgment it is unwise for the court or the EAT to set out guidelines, and wrong to make rules and establish presumptions for industrial tribunals to follow or take account.'

These decisions of the Court of Appeal have been seen as part of the attack on 'legalism' in tribunal cases.

7 Termination of the contract of employment – special categories

You should be familiar with the following areas:

- dismissals which are automatically fair
- requirements of dismissals which are automatically fair
- dismissals which are automatically unfair
- requirements of dismissals which are automatically unfair
- remedies for dismissals which are automatically unfair

Dismissals which are automatically fair

National security

A minister of the Crown may issue a certificate that specified employment be excluded from the protection of unfair dismissal protection in order to safeguard national security (*Council of Civil Service Union v Minister for Civil Service* (1985)).

Dismissal during a strike or a lock-out

An industrial tribunal cannot determine whether a dismissal is fair or unfair, if at the date of dismissal:

- the employer was conducting or instituting a lock-out; or
- the employee was taking part in a strike or other industrial action.

Unless it can be shown that either:

- one or more of the relevant employees of the same employer has not been dismissed; or

- that such an employee has before the expiry of the period of three months beginning with the employees date of dismissal, been offered re-engagement, and that the employee concerned has not been offered re-engagement.

Note
These exceptions do not apply if the strike is unofficial; dismissals may then be selective.

If there is a selective dismissal or selective re-engagement within three months, this does not mean that the dismissal is automatically unfair; it means that the industrial tribunal may investigate in the usual way whether the dismissal is fair, having regard to equity and the circumstances of the case. The employer would have to show that his selection criteria were fair, and that the dismissal was for one of the potentially fair grounds.

An employee who is taking part in an unofficial strike has no right at all to bring a claim of unfair dismissal.

Requirements for an automatically fair dismissal

1 There must be:
  - a lock-out – ie the closing of a place of work, or the suspension of work, or the refusal by an employer to continue to employ any number of persons employed by him, in consequence of a dispute; or
  - a strike – Lord Denning defined a strike as a 'concerted stoppage of work by men, done with a view to improving their wages or conditions, or giving vent to a protest, or supporting other workmen'. An individual protest would not therefore qualify; or
  - other industrial action – this traditionally includes such techniques as a 'work-to-rule', a 'go-slow', or a 'sit-in'. It used to be assumed that a breach of contract had to be involved to establish some other industrial action. However, in *Power Packing Case Makers v Faust* (1983) it was held that three employees who had refused to work overtime in order to impose pressure in a pay dispute, had taken part in 'other industrial action' and were debarred from claiming unfair dismissal although they had no contractual obligation to work overtime. Other industrial action, like a strike, is essentially a collective rather than an individual activity.

In *Thompson v Eaton* (1976), employees were standing around a new machine in order to prevent the employer from using it; they were ordered back to work; they refused; and they were dismissed. Held: the dismissal was for taking part in industrial action.

Whether there was a strike or a lock-out, etc is a question of fact not of law.

2   It affects only relevant employees

In the case of a lock-out relevant employees are defined as employees who are directly interested in the dispute. It will include not only those who were locked out, but also any other employees who would be affected by the outcome of the dispute.

In *Fisher v York Trailer Co* (1991) the relevant employees were the seven who were actually locked-out and dismissed plus the 27 other employees who had agreed to continue to work at the normal pace.

In the case of a strike or other industrial action, relevant employees are those who are taking part at the date of dismissal.

3   They must have been taking part

- If the employee is sick or away on holiday and has not taken part in any way, then he has not participated (*Hindle Gears Ltd v McGinty* (1984)).

- But if, before his absence for sickness or on holiday, he had taken part, then he will still be considered as having taken part.

  In *Williams v Western Mail* (1980), an employee who took part in a one-day strike stayed away the next day owing to illness. Held: he had not stopped supporting the industrial action and was thus still taking part.

- A refusal to cross a picket line can prove to be difficult.

  In *McCormick v Horsepower Ltd* (1981), the Court of Appeal held that an engineer from another department who temporarily and individually refused to cross a picket line was not taking part in industrial action, as he was not acting in concert with the strikers' or anyone else.

  However, in *Coates v Modern Methods and Materials* (1982), Mrs Leith had turned up to go to work, but on encountering a factory gate meeting, she decided not to go in as she was frightened of abuse from her fellow workers. The Court of Appeal laid down an objective test – participation in a strike must be judged by what an employee does, not what he thinks, or why he does it. If he stops working when his work mates come out on strike, and does not do anything or say anything to make plain his disagreement with the strike, or what could amount to a refusal to join them; he takes part in the action.

- A genuine belief by the employer that the employee took part in the strike is not sufficient; it is up to the employer to prove that the employee participated.

- An employer must be careful not to dismiss before the strike began. In *Midland Plastics Ltd v Till* (1983), a letter was sent to the management stating that unless certain demands were met, industrial action would commence at 11 am. At 9.30 am the managing director dismissed four workers. Held: they were not taking part in industrial action.

- An employer must be careful not to dismiss after the strike has ended. In *Heath v Longman* (1973), employees went on strike but subsequently returned to work. One of them informed the employer that the strike was over, but when they returned to work, they were dismissed. Held: they were not on strike.

4   Re-engagement

- An employer may offer re-engagement on a selective basis three months after the date of dismissal.

- Even within the three-month period, he may offer re-engagement to different strikers on different terms. In *Williams v National Theatre Board Ltd* (1982) 30 men went on strike. One woman struck in sympathy for a few days and then went back to work. All were dismissed. The men were offered re-engagement on a second disciplinary warning basis; the woman was re-engaged without any warning. Held: it was for management to decide the terms of re-engagement.

- Re-engagement need not be offered to all employees at the same time. In *Highland Fabricators v McLaughlin* (1995), it was held that the tribunal had no jurisdiction where all employees had been offered re-engagement within three months, although in the original offer the claimant had been excluded, and the offer to him had only been made after he had found alternative employment.

- In *Bigham & Keogh v GKN Kwikform* (1992), the EAT held that for there to be an offer of re-employment of a dismissed striker, the employer must have actual or constructive knowledge of why the employee was dismissed from his first job. In this case, Mr Keogh had revealed that he had been employed at a different site, but did not reveal, and was not asked why he left. Held: there was a re-engagement.

Dismissals which are automatically unfair

Certain dismissals are termed automatically unfair. These include the following:

Dismissal for trade union membership or trade union activities

A dismissal on the above ground is automatically unfair. Since it is an essential part of the protection given to trade union members, details are included along with action short of dismissal and a prohibition on refusal to employ for the same reasons under the heading of 'Freedom of Association' in Chapter 9, pp 156–58.

Dismissals covered by The Transfer of Undertakings Regulations

It is essential, at this stage, that students return to Chapter 3 for a description of the qualifying transfers and the employees who are covered by the Regulations, see Chapter 3, pp 43–46.

When is the dismissal unfair?
Any dismissal caused by the transfer, or any reason connected with it, is automatically unfair.

It was held in *Milligan v Securicor* (1995) that two years' continuous employment is not necessary, but this has been overruled by s 5 of the 1995 Amending Regulations.

However, if it was for an 'economic, technical, or organisational reason entailing changes in the workforce' (ETO) it will be deemed fair on the ground of 'some other substantial reason'.

The House of Lords held in *Gorictree v Jenkinson* (1994) that, despite this, the employees may still claim a redundancy payment. ETO has not yet been interpreted by the ECJ. However, the Advocate General has given it as his opinion that it would only cover cases where dismissals would have taken place anyway without a transfer. This view has not been followed by the British Courts.

It was stressed in *Berriman v Delabole Slate Ltd* (1985) that for an ETO there must be a change in the workforce. Merely reducing an employee's pay in order to standardise employee benefits will not suffice. Similarly in *Wheeler v Patel* (1988) it was held that a dismissal by the transferor at the behest of the transferee in order to get a higher price for the business does not qualify as an 'economic' reason; the three words must be read together.

A change in the workforce requires either a change in numbers and/or a change in functions.

It does not always require a diminution in numbers. In *Crawford v Swinton Insurance Brokers Ltd* (1990) where a clerk was required to become an insurance sales man, it was held that this entailed a change in the workforce.

The transferred employee is in a better position than existing employees whose terms can be changed by a reorganisation which qualifies as 'some other substantial reason'. It is not clear when a dismissal ceases to be in connection with a transfer.

Which employer is liable?

- A pre-transfer dismissal not connected with the transfer – the transferor.
- A pre-transfer dismissal connected with the transfer – the transferee.
- A pre-transfer dismissal connected with the transfer but fair for EOT, but where redundancy payments have to be made, the transferee.
- A post-transfer dismissal connected with the transfer – the transferee.

Where the contract has been transferred by TUPE then the transferee alone will be responsible, although the draft directive does suggest joint liability.

Dismissal on the ground of pregnancy (s 99 of the ERA 1996)

See Chapter 3 for other pregnancy rights. Prior to 1994, it was automatically unfair to dismiss an employee on grounds of pregnancy, provided the employee had two years 'continuous service'; and unless she was incapable of doing the job she was employed to do, or continued employment would infringe a statutory provision. Now, however, those provisions have been superseded as follows.

An employee is deemed to be unfairly dismissed if the reason or the principle reason for the dismissal was:

- pregnancy, or any reason connected with the pregnancy;
- her maternity leave was ended by dismissal for reasons connected with the childbirth;
- she availed herself of maternity leave;
- she was dismissed within the four weeks after the end of her maternity leave;
- one of the requirements which gives rise to suspension on medical grounds;
- she was dismissed within the four weeks after the end of the maternity leave, and was covered at that time by a medical certificate;
- she was made redundant and was not offered suitable alternative work;
- she was selected for redundancy for one of the above reasons.

An employer who dismisses a pregnant woman while she is on maternity leave must give her a written statement of the reasons for the dismissal. A dismissal for one of the above reasons is an 'inadmissible dismissal' and does not therefore require a two-year period of continuous employment.

Note

1 The two exceptions in the EPCA have now been abolished.

   If a woman becomes incapable of working because of her pregnancy, then she will be entitled to sick leave on her usual contractual terms, or maternal leave in suitable circumstances. In *Brown v Rentokil* (1995), the Court of Session held that it was not sex discrimination to dismiss a woman for a pregnancy-related illness as a man absent through illness for the same amount of time would be dismissed. The House of Lords has referred this matter to the ECJ.

   If continued employment would be contrary to a Code of Practice or Statutory Enactment, she must be offered suitable alternative employment or be suspended on 'maternity grounds' (see Chapter 3, p 50).

2 A dismissal on the ground of pregnancy is also contrary to the SDA, see *Webb v EMO*, p 67.

3 In *O'Neill v Governors of St Thomas More RCVA School* (1996), the EAR ruled that the dismissal of a religious education teacher after it became generally known that she was pregnant by a Roman Catholic priest was on the grounds of pregnancy. This contrasts with the previous case of *Berrisford v Woodward School* (1991), where

it was held that a pregnant teacher who had indicated that she would not be getting married was dismissed on the ground of morality rather than pregnancy. It was not discriminatory because a male teacher would have been dismissed in the same circumstances.

Health and safety (s 100 of the ERA 1996)

It is automatically unfair to dismiss (or to subject to any other detriment):

- Any person on the grounds that:

  (a) he left, or proposed to leave his place of work in circumstances of serious or imminent danger; or

  (b) he took or proposed to take appropriate steps to protect himself or other employees in circumstances of serious or imminent danger.

- Employees who have a specific responsibility for health and safety on the grounds that:

  (a) they carried out activities in connection with health and safety which they had been designated to carry out; or

  (b) they carried out functions in connection with their position as safety representatives, or members of safety committees.

It is also automatically unfair to select employees for redundancy on any of the above grounds. Such dismissals are termed inadmissible, and therefore do not require a qualifying period of two years, there is no age limit, the exclusion of tribunal jurisdiction for dismissal while on strike, etc do not apply and there is enhanced compensation, a special award and a possibility of interim relief (see Chapter 8).

Asserting a statutory right

It is automatically unfair to dismiss an employee if the reason for the dismissal was that the employee brought proceedings to enforce certain statutory rights or alleged in good faith that his employer had infringed one of those rights.

The relevant statutory rights are:

- any right under the ERA 1996, for which the remedy is a complaint to an industrial tribunal;

- the right to require an employer to stop deducting union subscriptions, or contributions to a unions political fund;

- minimum notice requirements under the ERA 1996;
- the right to complain of action short of dismissal on grounds related to union membership or union activities;
- the right to time off for trade union duties and activities.

Again the normal two-year qualification period and the age limits do not apply.

Other automatically unfair dismissals

Special protection is also given to:
- employees who refuse to work on Sunday (Chapter 3);
- employees appointed as member trustees of pension funds;
- employees appointed as employee representatives for consultation on redundancies or the transfer of undertakings.

Normal qualifying periods are not required for any of the above; and trustees of pension funds and employee representatives also qualify for enhanced compensation, a special award and interim relief (see Chapter 8).

8 Termination of the contract of employment – remedies

You should be familiar with the following areas:

- the statutory remedies for unfair dismissal
- the entitlement to redundancy payments
- the calculation of redundancy payments
- some observations on unfair dismissal and redundancy payments

Remedies for unfair dismissal (ss 111–32 of the ERA 1996)

Reinstatement and re-engagement

A tribunal which has found that the claimant was unfairly dismissed must ask him whether he wishes to be reinstated or re-engaged.

Reinstatement means that the employee is fully restored to his former position as if he had not been dismissed, eg arrears of pay, pay rises, seniority are all restored.

Re-engagement is more flexible. It can be re-engagement by the employer, a successor or an associate employer in a comparable job. The tribunal can use its discretion with regard to the restoration of any benefit.

If he wishes to be re-employed, then the tribunal must consider:

- Whether re-employment is practicable

  It is for the employer to show that re-employment is impracticable It could arise from the unfitness or inability or unsuitability of the claimant to do the work (*Rao v Civil Aviation Authority* (1994)); opposition to his return from the workforce (*Coleman v Magnet Joinery Ltd* (1975)); the breakdown of personal relationships in a small firm (*Enessy Co SA v Minoprio* (1978)).

The appointment of a permanent replacement may not be taken into account unless the employer can show that the work could only be done by a permanent replacement, or that the permanent replacement was appointed after a reasonable lapse of time without the claimant notifying his wish to be re-employed.

• Whether the claimant caused or contributed to the dismissal, in which case the tribunal must consider whether it would be just to order re-engagement.

If the tribunal does order re-engagement, and the employer fails to comply, this does not amount to contempt of court. Instead the tribunal must order compensation to be paid together with additional compensation for the failure to comply (see below).

However, at this stage the employer has a second opportunity to show that re-employment is impracticable. In *Port of London Authority v Payne* (1994) the Court of Appeal stated that the original judgment could be judged afresh at this stage; that re-engagement should be judged on the basis of practicability not possibility, and that the commercial judgment of the employer must be taken into account. They held that the decision that re-engagement was practicable because the employer could have asked for volunteers for redundancy was incorrect.

In practice, reinstatement or re-engagement are rarely ordered; a recent survey places it as 1% of decided cases. Re-employment is sometimes termed the 'lost remedy'.

Compensation

The government announces each September any increase in the statutory limits on compensation. The figures used here are those in force in July 1997.

Compensation consists of:

1 A basic award

This is calculated in the same way as a redundancy payment. It is based on three factors – the age of the claimant, the length of continuous employment, the weekly pay of the claimant.

Age	Weeks pay for each year of employment
18–21	0.5
22–40	1.0
41–65	1.5

No account is taken of

- any service beyond 20 years;
- any week's pay above £210.

The maximum basic award is therefore £6,300.

The basic award may be reduced by the amount of any redundancy money that has been paid. In addition, it may be reduced to such extent as the tribunal considers just and equitable, eg if the employee has unreasonably refused an offer of reinstatement or re-engagement; or if the employees conduct prior to the dismissal justifies it.

2 Compensatory award

This is based on the estimated loss sustained by the claimant. The tribunal will specify the amount under the following headings:

- immediate loss of wages;
- future loss of wages;
- loss of benefits;
- expenses in seeking work;
- loss of pension rights;
- loss of future employment protection;
- manner of dismissal.

Certain deductions must be made from the compensatory award:

- The claimant must mitigate his loss so far as possible, eg by taking reasonable steps to find other employment. If he fails to do so, the award may be reduced.

  In *Bessenden Properties v Corness* (1977), the claimant turned down an offer of employment. The Court of Appeal stated the test was 'where the applicant had no hope of recovering compensation from anyone else, and if he had considered merely his own interest, and had acted reasonably in all the circumstances, would he have accepted the job'?

- The tribunal may reduce the award to such extent as it considers 'just and equitable' if it considers that the employee caused or contributed to his dismissal.
- The amount by which any redundancy payment exceeds the basis award, may be taken from the compensatory award.
- Unemployment benefit may be recovered by the DHSS – but not if a settlement is reached out of court.

The compensatory award is subject to a maximum of £11,300.

3   Additional compensation for a failure to re-engage or reinstatement.

- In cases of race or sex discrimination 26–52 weeks' pay (based
  on a maximum of £210 a week).
- In other cases of unfair dismissal – 13–26 weeks' pay (based on
  a maximum of £210 a week).

4   Special award

In cases of unfair dismissal on the ground of trade union membership, etc health and safety activities, assertion of a statutory right,
employee representatives and pension trustees there are special
provisions. Such awards are calculated as follows:

- Basis award – here subject to a minimum of £2,700
- Compensatory award – calculated in the usual way
- Special award

    (a) Where reinstatement or re-engagement is not ordered, a
    weeks pay multiplied by 104, or £13,775, whichever is the
    greater. This award is subject to a maximum of £27,500.

    (b) Where an industrial tribunal has made an order for rein-
    statement or re-engagement of the dismissed employee, and
    the employer does not comply therewith – a week's pay mul-
    tiplied by 156, or £20,600, whichever is the greater sum.
    There is no maximum in this case.

The award is subject to a reduction if the employee is nearing retirement, or is responsible for conduct which makes deduction just and
equitable or has unreasonably prevented the reinstatement order
being complied with.

Note
Where pressure is put on an employer by a Trade Union or its members to dismiss non-unionists where there is a closed shop agreement,
the employer may request the trade union or the person exercising the
pressure to be joined in the proceedings. If compensation is awarded –
the tribunal may order the trade union or other person exercising the
pressure to pay all or part of the compensation.

Interim relief

If a dismissal is alleged to be for trade union membership, or non-
membership, or trade union activities, or any of the other above reasons qualifying for interim relief, the tribunal may order that the

claimant be retained in employment, and his contractual benefits preserved until the hearing of the claim. The application to the tribunal must be supported by a certificate signed by an official of a trade union to the effect that there are reasonable grounds for believing that the dismissal was on these grounds.

Redundancy payments

Redundancy payments were first introduced by the Redundancy Payments Act 1965 and it was the first provision to entitle workers to a payment when they lost their jobs. It is said to have led inevitably to the unfair dismissal payments six years later.

The aims of the act have been variously described as:

- rewarding long service;
- giving an employee a property right in his job;
- promoting job mobility in a time when the old heavy industries were running down and new technologies were emerging;
- improving industrial relations by rendering strikes over job losses less likely.

Whatever its original aims, it has recently been described as itself redundant due to the low nature of the payments available. The compensation for unfair dismissal is considerable higher as are many private redundancy schemes run by various organisations.

Statutory redundancy provisions are now be found in ss 135–65 of the ERA 1996.

Qualifications for bringing a claim

In considering the cases on redundancy, it is important to remember that before 1971 it was to the employees advantage to prove that they were redundant, as this was the only way they could obtain compensation for losing their jobs. Since 1971, however, employees tend to argue that they were not redundant as this might lead to a higher unfair dismissal compensation.

To be entitled to a redundancy payment, an employee:

- must not be disqualified from bringing a claim;
- must have completed a 'qualifying period' of 'continuous employment';

- must have been dismissed; and
- the dismissal must have been due to a redundancy.

Persons disqualified form bringing a claim

- Persons who have attained the normal retiring age (see Chapter 6, for meaning of 'normal retiring age') or the age of 65.
- Employees who are entitled to an occupational pension of periodic payment or a lump sum may be served a notice by the employer that his right to a redundancy payment is excluded or reduced. If the annual value of the pension is equal to one-third of the employee's leaving salary and is payable immediately, the employer may exclude altogether the right to receive a redundancy payment. If the pension is less than one-third or is not payable immediately but within 90 weeks, the redundancy payment is reduced proportionately.
- As for unfair dismissal – see Chapter 6, pp 107–10.

Continuous employment

As for unfair dismissal – see Chapter 3, pp 39–43.

Continuous employment is particularly important for redundancy payments as it governs not only entitlement but also the amount of the redundancy payment.

Dismissal

- Dismissal ordinarily means dismissal as in 'unfair dismissal' (see Chapter 6, pp 111–13).

'Jumping the gun' is a major problem in the case of redundancies. In *Morton Sundour Fabrics v Shaw* (1966) Shaw was warned that his job was likely to end at some time in the future. He immediately found another job and left. Held: no dismissal.

Special arrangements have however been made for an employee under notice who wishes to leave early; he must serve an 'anticipatory notice' on his employer; if the employer does not object, the employee may leave early and retain his right to redundancy payments. If, however, the employer requests him to withdraw his 'anticipatory notice', and he refuses to do so and leaves, then the question of redundancy payments must be decided by the industrial tribunal.

If an employee during the period of notice goes on strike and is dismissed for doing so, he is still entitled to redundancy payments.

Employees on strike during period of notice may be required to return to work to work the number of days of notice lost during the strike.

- Where an employee has been laid off (without pay) or put on short time (entitled to less than half a week's pay) for at least four consecutive weeks or for any six weeks out of a period of 13 weeks, this entitles the employee:

(a) to serve notice, claiming a redundancy payment; and

(b) to terminate the employment.

The employer may serve counter-notice if he believes that there is a reasonable prospect of resuming normal working.

Entitlement to redundancy payment will then be considered by a tribunal.

- An employee volunteers for redundancy – provided the initial approach comes from the employer.

No dismissal

- Where the employee accepts an offer of alternative employment with the employer, or an associated employer, or a new owner of the business, and the new contract starts immediately or within four weeks of the ending of the old contract.

If the new renewed contract differs in any way from the previous contract, the first four weeks of work under the contract are regarded as a trial period. (A longer trial period may be agreed for the purpose of retraining the employee.)

If the employee terminates the contract during the trial period or is dismissed for any reason concerned with the new employment, he is treated as having been dismissed at the end of the previous contract and entitled to redundancy payments.

- Where the employee unreasonably refuses an offer of re-engagement in the same or suitable alternative employment. Whether the alternative employment is suitable must be judged objectively – looking at the nature of the work, the hours, the pay, the conditions, qualifications and experience.

In *Taylor v Kent CC* (1969) a headmaster became redundant when his school was amalgamated with another. He was offered alternative employment in a mobile pool of teachers covering staff shortages in another part of the county. Held: not suitable alternative employment because of the change in status.

There was a similar finding in *O'Brien v Associated Fire Alarms* (1969) because of a change in location.

In *Thomas Wragg v Wood* (1976), the EAT considered the fact that the offer had been made very late in the day; the employee had already accepted other work; he also feared that the offer would be temporary.

In considering 'suitable alternative employment' – the court looks at the jobs (objective). In considering 'unreasonably refused' – court looks at personal matters (subjective).

Redundancy
This occurs when an employee is dismissed because:

• The employer has ceased to carry on the business for which the employee was employed.

The tribunal may not go behind the decision to inquire whether it was necessary to close down.

In *Moon v Homeworthy Furniture* (1977) employees made redundant when a factory closed claimed that it had not been closed for economic reasons – but as a retaliatory measure by the employer because it had a bad industrial relations record. EAT declined to examine the reasons for the company's decision.

• The employer has ceased to carry on business at the place where the employee was employed.

In *UK Atomic Energy Authority v Claydon* (1974), it was held this means the place 'where under his contract of employment he could be required to work'. This contractual approach, however, was challenged in *Bass Leisure Ltd v Thomas* (1994), where the EAT held that the tribunal should ascertain the employee's normal place of work on a factual basis regardless of whether the contract required the employee to move from one place to another.

If there is no mobility clause in the contract, the courts will be reluctant to imply one (see *O'Brien v Associated Fire Alarms Ltd* (1969)).

Note

Even if there is no mobility clause – the employee may still be denied a redundancy payment if the offer of employment elsewhere is seen as an offer of suitable alternative employment. See also *Nelson v BBC* (1980); *United Bank v Akhtar* (1989); *White v Reflecting Roadstuds Ltd* (1991) (see Chapter 3, p 26).

- The employer's *need for employees* to carry out work of a particular kind has ceased or diminished.

There is a redundancy, where the work has not ceased or diminished, but:

- Independent contractors have been appointed to carry out the work (the need for employees has diminished) (see *Bromby & Hoare v Evans* (1972)).

- The employer needs to cut his salary bill.

    In an early case it was held that this did not amount to a redundancy. But in *AUT v University of Newcastle* (1987), where a lecturer was dismissed when funding was withdrawn, it was argued that there was no redundancy as the work still remained to be done. The EAT held, however, that the requirements of businesses are defined solely by the employer and here it had been decided that the lecturer was not necessary – there was therefore a redundancy.

- The work has been re-organised and shared amongst a number of employees – with the result that some employees are dismissed. In *Robinson v BI Airways* (1978) two posts disappeared after a re-organisation of tasks, and were replaced by one new post. Held: there were two redundancies.

- The work has increased – but it can be done by fewer employees by new improved means, eg mechanisation.

There is no redundancy, however, where:

- The work remains, but it is to be performed at a different time, ie tasks remain the same – but there are changes in the terms and conditions of employment. See *Lesney Products v Nolan* (1977) where employees had worked a long day shift with a lot of overtime in the evenings. The employers replaced this arrangement by two day shifts which meant that the weekly pay of employees was reduced by roughly a third. Held: no redundancy.

    Similarly in *Johnson v Notts Combined Police Authority* (1974), clerks who had worked normal office hours were required to work a two shift system. They refused and were dismissed. Held: no redundancy – although there was a change in the contract, they were not entitled to redundancy payments.

    But night shift as opposed to day shift work may be work of a particular kind, see *MacFisheries Ltd v Findlay* (1985).

- The demands of the job have changed, and the employee fails to adapt to new working methods. In *North Riding Garages Ltd v*

Butterwick (1967), a workshop manager with 30 years' experience was dismissed following a take-over and reorganisation of the business. The manager found it difficult to adapt to new methods in particular coping with costs estimates. Held: no redundancy the firm still needed a workshop manager. Butterwick could not adapt to the changing needs of job. See also *Hindle v Percival Boats* (1969).

It is sometimes difficult to decide whether there is a different job or whether it is the same job but the demands of the job have changed. The court concentrates on the characteristics of the job, rather than the aptitudes of the employee. In *Vaux Breweries v Ward* (1968), after the refurbishment of a pub, the employer decided to replace barmaids with bunny girls. Held: no redundancy – the requirements of the work had not changed merely the kind of employee favoured by the employer.

However, in *Murphy v Epsom College* (1985) the employee had been employed as a general plumber. The heating system was upgraded by introducing an electronic control system. Murphy was made redundant and replaced by a heating technician. Held: there was a redundancy – the new employee as doing a different job.

The distinction between a strict contractual approach and a job function test has also emerged in connection with whether the employee can be required to do a different job (as with a geographical mobility clause).

In *Nelson v BBC* (1977) the contract test was invoked. The employee described as 'Producer Grade 3' was able to deny he was redundant when the Caribbean Service was closed down.

In *Cowen v Haden* (1983) the employee was employed as divisional contracts surveyor but could be asked to do 'any and all duties which reasonably fell within his capabilities'. When his post disappeared in a reorganisation, he argued that he could not be regarded as redundant unless the employers could show that there was no other work within his capabilities. The Court of Appeal held that these words had to be related to the post of divisional contracts surveyor and that he was therefore redundant.

Reduction for misconduct

Under the s 140 of the ERA – if the employee commits an act of misconduct which at common law would entitle the employer to terminate the contract without notice, the employee will be disentitled to a redundancy payment. This is a total disqualification.

In *Sanders v Earnest Neale Ltd* (1974), the employees conducted a work-to-rule. The employer sacked them and the factory closed down. Held: it was not a dismissal for redundancy. The dismissals had led to the closing of the factory – not the other way round.

There are two exceptions:

- If the employee takes part in a strike or other industrial action whilst on notice for redundancy and is dismissed, the employee remains entitled to his redundancy payments. The employer can, however, serve a notice of extension on the employee after the end of the strike requiring him to work the number of days lost through the strike; if he refuses he loses redundancy pay.

- But in *Simmons v Hoover* (1977) a strike of some months caused a contraction in the employer's business. The employer dismissed the employees on the ground of redundancy. Simmons claimed a redundancy payment. Held: he was not entitled. This exception applies only to employees going on strike after a redundancy has been declared. In *Bonner v Gilbert Ltd* (1989), an employee while under notice of redundancy was dismissed for suspected dishonesty. The EAT held that the test was whether the employee was guilty not the employer's belief in his guilt.

Under s 92(3) if the employee commits any other form of misconduct whilst on notice for redundancy, the tribunal may award him such part of his redundancy payment as it considers to be just and equitable.

Payments

Responsibility rests with the employer.

If there is a dispute, a complaint may be made to the industrial tribunal within six months of dismissal.

Amount of payment:

For each year of employment between:

18–21	0.5 week's pay
22–41	1 week's pay
42–64	1.5 week's pay

For men and women over 64 there is a reduction of one-twelfth in the total entitlement in respect of each month over that age, so that entitlement ceases entirely on reaching 65.

All payments are subject to a maximum of 20 years' reckonable employment.

All payments are also subject to a maximum week's pay which is altered each year to meet inflation (at present £210 per week).

Maximum payment possible: 20 x 1.5 x 145 = weeks pay
For calculation of weeks pay see Chapter 3, pp 47, 48.

Unfair dismissal and management prerogative

It has been argued that despite its perceived aim of protecting the
rights of employees, the unfair dismissal provisions do in fact embody
a strong element of management prerogative, ie management's right
to hire and fire and to organise or reorganise a business.

Arguments against:

• Certain dismissals are automatically unfair.

   For example, dismissals on the ground of union membership or activities, sex, race, pregnancy, transfer of an undertaking, asserting a
   statutory right. Health and safety.

• In other cases employer has to establish that the dismissal is for one
   of five fair grounds; see pp 113–22.

• In all cases, employers must follow a fair procedure.

Arguments for strong element of management prerogative.

• Dismissal must be reasonable in the circumstances.

   The standard used is that of employers generally, not an objective
   standard set by the tribunal. See *Iceland Frozen Foods v Jones*
   (Chapter 6, p 123) where it was held that a tribunal must decide
   whether the dismissal was within the range of responses of a
   reasonable employer.

   Hugh Collins points out that the word 'range' broadens the scope
   for legitimate disciplinary action, and that the tribunals requirement that the employers action was 'unreasonable' rather than 'reasonable' again broadens the scope.

• Even with regard to specific grounds, reasonableness is examined
   from the employer's viewpoint not from whether it is unjust to the
   employee. See *BHS v Burchell; Monie v Coral* – above; dismissal on
   the ground of illness.

• The reason for the dismissal must be established, but 'some other
   substantial reason' is deliberately expressed in wide terms and
   interpreted widely by the court. It has been argued that almost any
   ground will do, eg *Saunders v National Camps* above.

   Particularly important for management prerogative is the employer's right to reorganise (*Hollister v NFU*); the employer's freedom to

change the contract of employment provided certain procedures are followed (*RS Components v Urwin*).

- The court will not examine the need for a redundancy, only the procedures used.

Collins argues that these factors create a presumption of fairness, and an excuse for non-intervention. The tribunals endorse the practices of management. The Court of Appeals statement in *Bailey v BP Oil* (1980) means that tribunals cannot enunciate their own standards; they can only reach a decision on the facts.

He also points out that the juridification of employment relationship runs deeply contrary to the settled values of the common law. The judiciary is required to abandon its traditional neutrality, and to protect job security. They have shown themselves to be reluctant to do this.

The importance of contractual principles

It is also argued that the statutory protection for unfair dismissal has been diluted by the importation of common law contractual principles. For example:

- There must be a valid contract in the first place. If for instance the contract is void for illegality, there can be no claim of unfair dismissal.

- Constructive dismissal is dependent on a breach of contract by the employer. *Western Excavating v Sharp*, although the effect of this has been lessened to a certain extent by the development of the implied term of good faith.

- The employees implied duty to obey has been influential in respect of dismissals on the ground of misconduct.

- It is argued that the reluctance of the tribunals to order reinstatement or re-engagement arises from the common law practice of refusing specific performance for contracts of employment.

- The employer may also influence the position through his drafting of the contract in the first place, ie:

  (a) he may devise his arrangements in such a way that it becomes a contract for services (self-employed) rather than a contract of service;

  (b) he will draft the disciplinary arrangements.

  He may identify the offences which will amount to gross misconduct which may therefore lead to dismissal without previous warnings.

A new model

Hugh Collins has suggested an alternative controversial model for unfair dismissal legislation. He has suggested that dismissal should be classified as follows.

Disciplinary dismissals – which would involve some misconduct or incompetence or inability on the part of the employee.

The procedures would be more or less the same as at present.

Economic dismissals – which would cover both redundancy dismissals under the present system, and also reorganisation of the business which currently qualifies as 'some other substantial reason'. He suggests that this category should include any dismissal for a business reason unconnected with the behaviour of the employee. He does not consider that any compensation should be payable by the employer in these circumstances.

Public rights dismissals – which would cover not only dismissals on the grounds of race, sex or trade union membership but also age, religion, political views and sexual orientation. It should also incorporate the right to strike, and right to free speech. They should all qualify for enhanced compensation.

Collins argues that it is where the current arrangements depart from this model that they are seen as unsatisfactory.

9 Trade unions and their members

You should be familiar with the following areas:

- the status of trade unions
- freedom of association as it affects employers
- freedom of association as it affects trade unions
- enforcing members rights

On the one hand, trade unions are voluntary unincorporated associations, and so belong to the same legal category as, for example, tennis clubs, and their leaders have from time to time claimed for them the same unhampered control over their own affairs as a tennis club. On the other hand, in reality there are considerable differences between trade unions and tennis clubs; trade unions wield considerable political and economic influence; their decisions have considerable impact on the working life of British people and trade union membership may be an important factor in securing access to or retaining a job. Trade union representatives sit on commissions, committees and tribunals; the effect of collective bargaining is sometimes socially indistinguishable from legislation; unions participate in the making of rules and norms which affect a large proportion of the population.

The law reflects this reality because legislation has increasingly intervened to regulate the internal affairs of trade unions.

The status of a trade union

Definition

Section 1 of the TULR(C)A defines a trade union as:

An organisation (whether permanent or temporary) which either:

- consists wholly or mainly of workers of one or more descriptions whose principal purposes include the regulation of relations between workers and employers, or

- consists wholly or mainly of organisations described above or their representatives.

Note
The definition covers individual trade unions and confederated organisations, eg Confederation of Shipbuilding and Engineering Unions; or the Trades Union Congress.

'Workers' is a term wider in import than employee. It can include the self employed, provided they are obliged by their contract to offer their personal services. It does not, however, cover professional organisations such as the Law Society, or those who sell a work of some kind, eg authors working for the BBC. 'Purposes include' other purposes including political objects may also be included. These are however, subject to strict statutory controls.

Form of association

Section 10 of the TULR(C)A provides that a trade union shall not be a body corporate, but shall nonetheless be capable of making contracts; suing and be sued in its own name, and be prosecuted in its own name. Its property will be held by trustees on its behalf.

Special Register Bodies, ie professional bodies whose principal purposes include labour management relations, eg Royal College of Nursing, may however retain their corporate status.

Listing

The Certification Officer maintains a list of trade unions.

Accounting records

Any trade union which has been in existence for at least a year must keep accounting records providing a true and fair view of the unions affairs, and make annually to the Certification Officer a return of its financial affairs of the previous calendar year, audited by qualified officers. Penalties are imposed for non-compliance.

Certificate of independence

A trade union that is on the list may apply to the Certification Officer for a certificate that it is an independent trade union.

A union is independent if:

- it is not under the domination or control of an employer or a group of employers, or an employers association; and

- it is not liable to interference by an employer or any such group or association arising out of the provision of financial or material support or by any other means whatsoever tending towards such control.

In *Squibb UK Staff Association v Certification Officer* (1979), the Court of Appeal held that the above wording prohibited an organisation which was 'vulnerable to interference' rather than 'likely in fact to be interfered with'. In that case the union was so reliant on the employers support that it could not continue without it. It was refused a certificate of independence.

The Certification Officer set out the following criteria for deciding whether a union was independent.

- History – was it set up by management with management help?

  In *Blue Circle Staff Association v CO* (1977), the EAT approved of the Certification Officers criteria and confirmed that a staff association set up six months previously by the employer with total employer control ('a sophisticated instrument of personnel control') was not independent.

- Finance – if a union receives a subsidy from an employer, it is unlikely to be classified as independent.

- Facilities – if the employer subsidises the union by providing free office space, free mail and telephones, free meeting place, free photocopying as in the *Squibb* case then the union is unlikely to be independent. Note, however, that the ACAS Code of Practice advises that employers should make available to union officials the facilities which they need to perform their duties efficiently.

- Attitude – a lack of a 'robust attitude in negotiation' may indicate a lack of independence.

- Membership – if membership is limited to one company this may indicate a lack of independence. It is not an absolute bar to independence, however, see NUM.

- Rules – in *Blue Circle* the employers nominated the chair of the Joint Central Committee; in addition management representatives had originally been members of the committee and had helped to draw up the rules which removed them in order to apply for a certificate of independence.

In *Government Communications Staff Federation v CO* (1993), the EAT held that the federation was liable to interference as the Director of GCHQ could withdraw his approval for their existence.

An appeal lies to the EAT against a refusal by the Certification Officer to grant a Certificate.

Most of the rights give to trade unions or to trade union members are given only to trade unions in receipt of a certificate of independence.

Freedom of association

This is considered a fundamental human right which appears in international declarations and covenants such as the Universal Declaration of Human Rights 1948; The European Convention of Human rights; the EU Social Chapter as well as in a number of constitutions. It appears alongside other freedoms such as freedom of speech, freedom of religion, freedom from arbitrary arrest.

It involves:

- an absence of prohibitions;
- the presence of positive guarantees.

Absence of prohibition

The first essential is freedom from criminal restraint, but this does not guarantee that its exercise will not be impeded by social forces, eg employers or the unions themselves.

The UK was one of the first countries in Europe to lift the ban on trade unions.

- The Combination Law Repeal Act 1824 removed the criminality of trade unions by neutralising the common law of criminal conspiracy, and confirmed the repeal of earlier statutory provisions against combinations.

- The Trade Union Act 1876 removed finally the illegal nature of trade unions. Until then, although not criminal, they were still illegal as organisation in restraint of trade, and their agreements were thus unenforceable.

At no time since has this freedom of association been impaired except:

- In the case of the armed forces who are not permitted to join a trade union.

- Between 1927–46 established civil servants were not allowed to be members of any organisation unless its membership was restricted to crown servants, and it was not affiliated to any outside organisation.

- Since the Police Act 1919, members of the police force have not been free to join trade unions.

- In 1984, employees at GCHQ were prohibited from joining trade unions on the ground of securing national safety, but this prohibition was removed by the labour government in 1997.

Until recently there was a glaring contrast between the wide scope of this freedom, and the absence of any legislation to guarantee its exercise.

Positive guarantees against employers

Early protection

- 'Fair wages' clauses were inserted into government or other public authority contracts which made it a condition of the contract, license or subsidy, that the employer and subcontractor used union labour. This was repealed in 1982.

- The Industrial Relations Act 1971 proclaimed that for the first time in this country freedom of organisation as a legal principle, ie the freedom to be a member of a trade union and to participate in its activities, and to stand or to hold office. If an employer infringed this principle, this would be an unfair industrial practice, and compensation would be payable to the employees concerned. These rights however, were only granted to 'registered' trade unions, and since most trade unions refused to register, the provision was not of practical importance, even before the act was repealed in 1974.

The present situation

Lord Wedderburn has stated that 'a right to associate has been built on the building blocks of individual rights'. However, in recent years, these building blocks have been weakened.

The individual rights concerned are:

- the right to paid time off for union duties, and unpaid time off for union activities (see Chapter 3, pp 57, 58);
- protection against dismissal, or action short of dismissal for trade union membership or trade union activities, and refusal to offer employment on the ground of trade union membership.

Dismissal for trade union membership or trade union activities

A dismissal on the above ground is automatically unfair and therefore:

- there is no qualifying period of continuous employment;
- there is no need to show that the dismissal is reasonable in the circumstances;
- there is no maximum age limit;
- an application for interim relief may be made within seven days of the dismissal, accompanied by a signed certificate from a union official that there is reasonable ground for believing that the dismissal is made on this ground. The tribunal may then make an order preserving the employees benefits under the contract, until the case is determined.

An order for damages will include in addition to the compensatory award:

- a minimum basic award of £2,700;
- where reinstatement or re-engagement is not ordered, a special award of 104 weeks' pay (minimum £13,775; maximum £27,500);
- where reinstatement or re-engagement is ordered but not complied with, 156 weeks' pay (minimum £20,600; there is no maximum in this case).

Where the employee is not qualified to bring a claim of unfair dismissal, then the burden of proof is on the employee.

This can be difficult as seen in *Smith v Hayle Town Council* (1978) where the applicant, the town clerk, was dismissed shortly after announcing that he was joining a trade union. His dismissal was approved by six votes to five in a council meeting. He was able to show that one of the councillors who had voted for his dismissal had done so on the ground of union membership, but was unable to establish the grounds for the other councillors actions. The Court of Appeal held that although there was an element of anti-unionism, this had not been proven to be the main reason for the decision.

The dismissal must have been on the ground of:

(a) trade union membership
For example carrying a union card.

In *Discount Tobacco Co Ltd v Armitage* (1990) the EAT considered that union membership extended to cover using the 'essential services of a trade union' such as invoking the assistance of a union official to obtain a written statement of the terms of employment. However, in *Associated Newspapers v Wilson* (1995) the House of Lords stated that membership of a union and using its services could not be equated. In that case, it was held that collective bargaining was not a union service.

It also originally covered membership of a particular trade union rather than just unions in general see *NCB v Ridgeway* (1987) where a member of the NUM was held to have been discriminated against because he was not awarded the same rise as members of the NUM, but see *Assoc Newspapers v Wilson* (below).

(b) trade union activities at an appropriate time
These have been held to cover:

- attending union meetings, acting as shop steward, attempting to recruit new members;
- activities in a previous employment.

In *Fitzpatrick v British Railways Board* (1992), Miss Fitzpatrick joined British Rail without disclosing that she had been dismissed from a previous employment on account of her disruptive union activities. When they discovered this, she was dismissed. The Court of Appeal held that the dismissal was due to the employers fear that she would repeat that behaviour in her current employment, and the dismissal was therefore on the ground of trade union activities.

They do not cover:

- taking part in industrial action;
- trade union type activities, which are not official trade union activities;

In *Chant v Aquaboats* (1978) an employee was dismissed for organising a petition complaining about safety at work. He was a member of a union, but the union had not asked him to organise a petition, and he was not an union official. It was not dismissal on the ground of trade union activities.

* actions specifically prohibited by union rules;
* the activity of a trade union, as distinct from the activity of union members;

In *Carrington v Thermastore* (1983) between 60 and 65 of the company's employees had joined the TGWU. The union had applied to the company for recognition. The company then asked a charge hand to select 20 employees for redundancy. All 20 were union members. The Court of Appeal held that the dismissal was in retaliation for the union action/activity, but was not related to what the individual employees had done. It was therefore not on the ground of trade union activity.

* activities at other than an appropriate time.

An appropriate time means outside working hours, or 'within working hours, in accordance with arrangements agreed with or consent given by the employer'.

In *Post Office v Union of Post Office Workers* (1974) the House of Lords held that working hours means any time when, in accordance with his or her contract of employment, he or she is required to be at work, and at work has been held to be actually working. This means that no permission is required for union activities during recognised breaks or before or after a working day. The House of Lords has inferred from this an entitlement for employees to take part in union activities on the employer's premises using facilities normally available to employees provided this does not cause any expense or inconvenience to the employer, or to employees who are not union members.

Consent may be implicit; but it was held in *Marley Tile Co v Shaw* (1980) that a union meeting was not held with the consent of the employer who had merely remained silent when he had been informed by an employee that he was going to a union meeting.

Action short of dismissal

Under ss 168, 169, 172 of the TULR(C)A 1992, every employee has a right not to have action short of dismissal taken against him by his employer for the purpose of preventing or deterring him from being a member of a trade union, or penalising him from doing so, or preventing or deterring him from taking part in the activities of a trade union at an appropriate time, or penalising him from doing so, or compelling him to become a member of a trade union.

'Membership of a trade union', and 'activities of a trade union' mean the same as they do with regard to the prohibition on dismissal.

Matters taken into consideration include:

- Purpose

  In *Gallagher v Dept of Transport* (1994) the employee had been allowed to spend all his working hours on trade union duties for some four years. He applied for promotion but was unsuccessful because his employers were not satisfied as to his managerial ability; he was advised to take a managerial post in order to show his capability; this would inevitably reduce his time on union activities. The Court of Appeal held that this request might have the effect of reducing his union activities, but that was not its purpose. Therefore there was no breach of this section.

  In *Associated Newspapers* the House of Lords confirmed that the fact that union membership may become less attractive as a result of the employers action did not necessarily mean that deterring union membership was its purpose.

- Action

  In *Associated Newspapers Ltd v Wilson* (1995), the company de-recognised the NUJ and entered into individualised contracts with employees. Those who entered the new contracts got a pay increase; those who wished to retain collective bargaining did not.

  Similarly, in *ABP v Palmer* (1995), employees who were prepared to enter individual contracts got higher pay increases than those who did not. In both cases, the Court of Appeal held that this contravened ASD: in both cases the employers purpose was to end collective bargaining, and this was likely to lead to a decrease in union membership. It discouraged union employees from being members of trade unions.

  Following this decision the government quickly added a new section to TURERA which was going through Parliament at that time. This provided that even if the employers intention is discriminatory, if it is also intended to further a change in the employers relationship with any class of employees the action will be permissible unless it was something which no reasonable employer would do.

  It has been suggested that this goes further than merely reversing the decision of the Court of Appeal, and that it could be used to justify preferring one union over another. However, this insert would now seem unnecessary in view of the House of Lords' decision. The House, on appeal, reversed the decisions of the Court of Appeal on the ground that 'action short of dismissal' will not cover an omission. This decision curtails significantly the protection given to employees. It means that refusing to union members a benefit given to other employees may not now be unlawful, even if the employers purpose is to discourage union membership. It overrules the decision in *NCB v Ridgeway*.

The House of Lords also considered whether the employers purpose had been unlawful. In the case of *Wilson*, the employers purpose had been to encourage as many employees as possible to sign up to the new contracts, thus avoiding any confusion, and the purpose in 'Palmer' was to encourage greater flexibility. In neither case did the House of Lords find any evidence that the purpose was to deter union membership.

Remedy

An action must be made to a tribunal within three months of action complained of. The tribunal may make a declaration that the statute has been breached, and may also award such compensation as it considers 'just and equitable'. The EAT has held that the employee must have suffered some injury as a result of the infringement: it has also suggested that injury should include non-pecuniary losses such as injury to health, or the frustration of a 'deep and sincere wish to join a union'.

Refusal of access to employment (s 137 of the TULR(C)A 1992)

It is unlawful for an employer to refuse to employ anyone on the grounds of trade union membership or non-membership. Originally it was proposed to give protection only to non-members, ie extending the prohibition on post entry closed shops to pre-entry closed shops. However, following the publication of the European Social Chapter it was decided to extend the same protection to unionists and non-unionists. The prohibition also extends only to cover trade union membership. Presumably there would be no problem if the employer had declined to appoint Miss Fitzpatrick.

The decision in *Beyer v Birmingham City Council* (1977) would be the same today. In that case a well-known union activist gained employment with the council by using a false name. When his real identity was discovered he was dismissed on the ground of misconduct. It was held that he was not protected because previous union activity was not protected. He would not be protected by s 137 either when seeking employment as 'union activity' is not covered.

Query – circulation of black-lists of union activists?

Freedom of association – positive guarantees against trade unions

Trade unions have also been reluctant in some cases to allows persons freely to join or have been quick to effect an expulsion. Legal intervention has also proved necessary in this area.

Right to join a trade union

At common law, there was no right to join a trade union. Lord Denning did try to establish a 'right to work'. In *Nagle v Fielden* (1966) in a case involving the Jockey Club's refusal to issue a licence to woman trainer on the ground of her gender, he stated that this right would be infringed if a body having a monopoly over the activity in question, refused admission without good reason.

He reiterated this view in *Edwards v Sogat* (1971), on the grounds that the closed shop interfered with a persons right to work when a trade union refused to re-admit him. Since Lord Denning's retirement, however, this has not been pursued.

Statutory provisions

Section 174 of the TULR(C)A 1992 now provides that unions may not exclude or expel someone except on one of four grounds:

* the applicant does not satisfy an enforceable membership criteria, eg employment in a particular trade or occupational group or having a particular qualification;
* he does not qualify on geographical grounds;
* he is no longer employed by the relevant employer;
* the exclusion or expulsion is attributable to his misconduct (does not cover resignation from another union, being a member of a particular political party, or unjustifiable discipline under s 65 – see below.

A complainant has the right to make a claim to an industrial tribunal within six months. If the complaint is well-founded, the tribunal makes a declaration and compensation can be awarded.

Discipline and expulsion

The courts have traditionally exerted some control over union expulsions and disciplinary procedures on the ground of breach of contract, and the rules of natural justice.

Breach of contract

The courts have interpreted the union's rule book as a contract between the members and the union. In *Lee v Showman's Guild of GB* (1952) where the union had fined a member £100 for 'unfair competition' the court held that whereas it would be bound by the internal tribunals finding of fact, it was for the court to decide whether the conduct complained of could constitute unfair competition.

Similarly in *Easterman v NALGO* (1974) the court decided that no reasonable domestic tribunal could have categorised the plaintiffs conduct as conduct which in the opinion of the branch committee renders her unfit for membership. (She had refused to take part in a strike designed to disrupt elections.)

The court will intervene on behalf of a member, if either:

* the rules are not followed; or
* the internal tribunal has not interpreted the rules properly.

The court will only declare a rule void if it is illegal or contrary to public policy, eg a rule attempting to exclude the jurisdiction of the court. *Lee v Showmans Guild of GB* (1952). However, a rule requiring a member to exhaust internal appeals before going to court will be upheld.

Natural justice

The rules of natural justice apply to the disciplinary powers of a trade union, ie a member is entitled to:

1 A right to be heard. This involves:

* Sufficient notice of the charge against him

    In *Annamunthodo v OWTU* (1961), the plaintiff knew that he was charged with making allegations against the union president, and knew that he could be fined. He did not know that he could be expelled. Held: the subsequent expulsion was void.

- An opportunity to present his case

There is no right to legal representation, or to an appeal.

2   The rule against bias

In *White v Kusych* (1951), the plaintiff was expelled from the union because of his opposition to the closed shop policy. The fact that those involved in the hearing had spoken out against that policy did not invalidate the decision. But in *Roebuck v NUM* (1978), two union officials had given evidence to a newspaper in a libel action taken by the union president, Mr Arthur Scargill, on behalf of the union. Mr Scargill presided over the hearing which recommended that the two officials be suspended from office for conduct prejudicial to the union, and then chaired the area council meeting which not surprisingly confirmed the decision. It was held that the suspension was void. Mr Scargill had been the complainant, and had made up his mind before the first hearing commenced, least of all the second.

Statutory provisions

For expulsion see also s 174 of the TULR(C)A 1992. In addition to the above actions at common law ss 164–67 of the TULR(C)A 1992 now creates a right not to be unjustifiably disciplined.

Disciplined is defined to include:

- expulsion;
- fines;
- refusal of access to any benefits;
- any other detriment.

Unjustifiable is defined to cover:

- failing to participate in industrial action;
- failing to contravene a provision in a contract of employment;
- asserting breaches of the regulations by an official or union representative, unless the assertion is made in bad faith;
- failing to agree or withdrawing agreement to deduction from wages of union fee;
- resigning or proposing to resign membership, or proposing to join or refusing to join another union;
- working with non-union members;
- working for an employer who employs non-union workers requiring the union to perform an act which by statute it must perform.

If the action complained of is an exclusion or expulsion under s 174, and the reason is a breach of s 165, the exclusion or exclusion is automatically unreasonable. In *NALGO v Courtney-Dunne* (1991) the EAT held that if a member is successful in obtaining a declaration and compensation, the union must put him in the position he was in before the unjustifiable discipline was imposed. The compensation awarded, should, however, reflect the loss suffered and should not be punitive.

In *Bradley v Nalgo* (1991) the complainant was expelled for not taking part in industrial action, and claimed compensation. The union did not contest the declaration, neither did it revoke the expulsion. The EAT awarded the minimum compensation only. The expulsion did not affect his job prospects nor his ability to join another union.

Commissioner for the Rights of Trade Union Members (CROTUM)

See Chapter 1, p 11.

10 Trade unions and employers – industrial relations

You should be familiar with the following areas:

- the nature of industrial relations
- the framework for collective bargaining
- the right to recognition
- the right to information
- the right to consultation
- Works Councils

Industrial relations

The principal function of a trade union is the conduct of industrial relations – the regulation of relations between its members and their employer. Traditionally, collective bargaining has been the central feature of British industrial relations, and British labour law has sought to provide an equilibrium between employers and workers in order to ensure the effective operation of a system of collective bargaining. This was associated with a policy of 'voluntarism' or 'abstentionism' or 'collective laissez faire' – whereby unions and employers were expected to make their own agreements; and patch-up their own quarrels with a minimum of state or legal interference.

Trade unions had a preference for collective bargaining even over supportive legislation:

- unions had obtained more advances through industrial strength than through reliance on the law;
- there was class antagonism to the judiciary;
- the common law had shown itself hostile to collectivism, preferring individual rights over collective power.

However, it has been argued that the law does have a role to play in industrial relations.

(a) It provides a floor of minimum rights for the individual employee (see Chapter 3).

(b) The law puts a ceiling on industrial action. Free collective bargaining implies the right to use the economic strength of the collective unit in order to secure the best possible bargain. The law defines what industrial action is permissible, and what is impermissible (see trade union immunities; see Chapter 11).

(c) The law buttresses and supports the system of collective bargaining by various props.

(d) The law can fill some of the gaps left in the system of collective bargaining by providing for the conditions of work of those workers who are inadequately unionised, and who cannot therefore properly participate in the system of collective bargaining, eg Wages Councils; Fair Wages Resolutions; s 11 of the EPA 1975 which allowed employers or trade unions to bring before the CAC employers who did not observe their general level of terms or conditions in a particular trade or industry. These were, however, all repealed between 1979 and 1987. Another device – contract compliance – was also rendered illegal.

(e) The law can create a framework for collective bargaining.

A right to recruit and organise is given by protecting the individual against victimisation for union membership or union activities, and by giving union officials time off to carry out their duties (see Chapter 9).

(f) The law encourages the peaceful settlement of disputes by offering facilities for conciliation, mediation, arbitration, etc.

(See Chapter 1 for the roles of ACAS and CAC.)

Collective bargaining

This most important feature of industrial relations is the process of collective bargaining. The wages and other conditions of employment of many workers are settled by some form of collective negotiations between their union or unions and their employer or employers. Traditionally the central purpose of British labour law was to ensure the effective operation of a system of collective bargaining.

However in recent years the emphasis has shifted.

- In 1991, the government in a Green Paper indicated its preference for individual bargaining over collective bargaining.
- ACAS and CAC remain as agencies to promote peaceful settlements of disputes, but ACAS's statutory duty to encourage the extension, development and reform of collective bargaining has been removed.
- Collective bargaining rights have been removed from teachers.
- Many of the props introduced for collective bargaining have been removed (see above).

It is argued that the following rights are required for effective collective bargaining.

The right to organise

See the freedom of association (Chapter 9).

This right which is exercised through a series of individual rights has been weakened in recent years.

The right to recognition

There is no legal right to recognition by an employer at present.

Unions must rely on persuasion, *cf*:

- 1974–80 when ACAS were granted power to investigate the views of employees and to order recognition where they considered this appropriate. The system did not work well; the provisions were complicated and weak, probably due to an ambivalence on the part of the labour government, and their reluctance to interfere too much with the voluntary system.
- In the US there is a legal duty to recognise and to bargain in good faith when the union membership reaches a certain level.
- In France, there is also a legal duty to negotiate.

Since 1980, recognition in the UK has been voluntary, but the present government has indicated that it will reintroduce a legal right to recognition.

The process of 'recognition' however, even if voluntary, is still of vital importance, as many rights depend on the trade union being recognised by the employer. It is necessary therefore to examine the exact meaning of 'recognition'.

Meaning of 'recognition'

Definition in TULR(C)A 1992: 'recognition of the union by the employer to any extent, for the purpose of collective bargaining.'

- There must have been an agreement between the employer and the union to negotiate on one or more of specified matters.
- The agreement may be express or implied. Most problems arise from alleged implied agreements.

In *NUGSAT v Albery Bros* (1979) the EAT stressed that recognition was an important step, and should not be assumed to have taken place without clear and unequivocal evidence, and usually a course of conduct over a period of time. It needs evidence of negotiation with a view to striking a bargain, a willingness merely to discuss would not suffice.

In *USDAW v Sketchley* (1981), the EAT rejected the argument that the union had been 'recognised' when the employer accepted union representative for disciplinary and grievance procedures, but not for negotiating terms and conditions of employment.

Note

1 Collective agreements are not legally enforceable, unless the contrary is stated in the agreement. An employer may therefore de-recognise a trade union.

2 There is no mechanism governing an employers choice of a recognised union. He may recognise a union which has minimal support in his organisation. Problems have arisen with single union deals, often on green-field sites, some negotiated before a single employee has been recruited.

The right to information

Section 181–85 of the TULR(C)A 1992 requires an employer to disclose to any recognised trade union, information without which the trade union would be, to a material extent, impeded in carrying out collective bargaining, and which is information which it would be in accordance with good industrial practice that he should disclose.

Note

1 The right is based on recognition, so employer can resist disclosure of certain information by refusing to bargain on that issue.

In *R v CAC, ex p BTP Tioxide Ltd* (1981), the union ASTMS had bargaining rights in respect of certain terms and conditions of employment, but in respect of a particular job evaluation scheme, it only had the right to make representations on behalf of its members seeking revaluation of their jobs, not the right to negotiate over the scheme itself. Because of this the Divisional Court held that the CAC had exceeded its jurisdiction in ordering disclosure by the employer of information relating to the scheme.

2   Collective bargaining must relate to matters set out in s 224 of the TULR(C)A 1992 – see p 186.

Information must relate to collective bargaining, not, eg to a company's investment strategy.

3   The ACAS Code of Practice gives examples of information which might be relevant, eg:

- pay and benefits (pay systems, job evaluation and grading schemes, total pay bill, fringe benefits);
- conditions of service (recruitment, training, promotion and redundancy policies, appraisal systems, health and safety matters);
- man-power (analysis of workforce, manpower and investment plans, any planned changes);
- performance (productivity, efficiency, and their savings, return on capital, state of order book);
- financial (cost-structure, gross and net profits, sources of earnings, assets, liabilities, allocation of profits, government aid, transfer prices, loans within a group, and interest charged).

4   Exceptions

Section 181 of the TULR(C)A 1992 enumerates the following exceptions:

- information conveyed to the employer in confidence;
- information relating specifically to an individual, eg individual salaries;
- information, the disclosure of which would cause substantial injury to the employer, eg customers would be lost, or suppliers would refuse to continue supplying.

Remedies for failure to supply information

(a) Union complains to CAC.

(b) CAC may:

- refer matter to ACAS for conciliation;
- itself conduct a hearing, after which it may make an order;
- if the order is not complied with, then the CAC may make an award on the terms and conditions of employment of the employee concerned, which will be incorporated into their contracts of employment.

Very few cases have been heard under this section.

It has been suggested that some unions are fearful that too much pressure in this area could lead to de-recognition. Some unions in any case believe that some information could inhibit a union, and that it is for management to manage , and how it gets itself into a position to meet the expectation of the employees is the management's problem, not the union's.

Note
Under the Companies Act, the Directors' Report in companies employing more the 250 employees must contain a statement describing what action has been taken to introduce, maintain, or develop a systematic dissemination of relevant information to employees, consultation with employees on matters likely to affect them, encouraging their involvement with the company through employee share schemes, and similar arrangements.

The right to consultation

Recognised trade unions have a statutory right to consultation in four circumstances:

- in relation to dismissals for redundancy (as a result of the Directive on Collective Redundancies);
- where there is a transfer of an undertaking (as a result of the Acquired Rights Directive);
- on health and safety matters;
- before contracting out of a state pension scheme.

The duty to consult on redundancies

This duty was altered on 1 March 1996, as a result of the Collective Redundancies and Transfer of Undertakings (Amendment) Regulations (1995). These were issued following the decision in *Commission of EC v UK* (1995) where the ECJ held that in limiting the right to consultation to *representatives of recognised trade unions* 'the UK was not complying with either Directive'.

An employer who proposes to dismiss 20 or more employees as redundant over a period of 90 days must consult 'appropriate representatives' of the threatened employees, ie either representatives elected by the threatened or affected employees or a representative of an independent trade union recognised for the group or category of employees to which the redundant employees belong.

The employee representatives may be elected on an *ad hoc* basis, as and when the redundancies are proposed, or under standing arrangements which may or may not relate specifically to redundancy or other situations.

The employer may choose to consult an employee representative even when he recognises a trade union.

Redundancy was redefined in 1993 to cover any dismissal which was not related to the individual concerned thus covering dismissals arising from a reorganisation or restructuring as well as from a 'downsizing'.

Consultation must take place regardless of whether it makes any difference.

When must consultation take place?

The employer must consult in 'good time' (instead of 'at the earliest opportunity') and:

(a) if 20–100 employees are to be dismissed in one establishment within 30 days, at least 30 days before the dismissal;

(b) if 100 or more employees are to be dismissed in one establishment within 90 days, 90 days before the dismissal.

'Establishment' is not defined.

In *Barratt v UCATT* (1978), employers proposed to dismiss 24 construction workers across eight sites which were administered from one location The EAT confirmed that they formed one 'establishment'. Associated employers, however, cannot constitute one employer for this purpose even where three companies shared accounting and personnel services, and were all subsidiaries of a holding company, as in *Green Ltd v ASTMS* (1984).

'Proposing to dismiss'

It was stated in *Hough v Leyland Daf Ltd* (1991) that the duty comes into effect once the employer has formed some view as to how many employees are to be dismissed, when it is to take place and how they are to be arranged. In that case, the EAT confirmed that a proposal had been formulated when a company's security manager made a firm recommendation that its security function should be contracted-out and was given the go-ahead to finalise the arrangements.

However, in *R v British Coal, ex p Vardy* (1993), Glidewell LJ pointed out that the wording in the directive differed from that in the Act. He pointed put that the directive requires consultation to begin when the employer is contemplating redundancies not when he is proposing them.

Consultation

To comply with the duty, the trade union or employee representative must be given the following information in writing:

- the reason for the proposal;
- the numbers and descriptions of the employees it is proposed to dismiss as redundant;
- the total number of employees of such description employed at the establishment in question;
- the proposed method of selecting the employees who are to be dismissed;
- the proposed method of carrying out the dismissals, including the period they are to take effect.

The original requirement was basically procedural. But in 1993, TUR-ERA added a duty to consult about:

- avoiding the dismissal;
- reducing the number of employees to be dismissed;
- mitigating the consequences of the dismissals.

The consultation must now be undertaken with a view to reaching agreement. It must take place in sufficient time before the notices are sent out. In *R v British Coal, ex p Price* (1992), the court stated that consultation should take place when plans are still at the formative stage.

Note
It is still consultation not negotiation.

Defence

An employer may be excused complying fully with the requirements. 'if there are special circumstances which render it not reasonably practicable for him to comply'.

In *Clarks of Hove Ltd v Bakers Union* (1978) 368 of 380 employees were summarily dismissed on the same day that the company ceased to trade, with no prior consultation. It had been in severe financial difficulties for some time. The Court of Appeal held that an insolvency which had been evident for some time was not 'special circumstances' under the Act. A sudden disaster such as destruction of the plant, or a trading boycott would qualify as 'special circumstances' but not ongoing financial problems.

Similarly it was held in *GMB v Rankin & Harrison* (1992) that shedding employees to make a company more attractive to a buyer is not something 'special', but a common incident in any form of receivership or insolvency.

However, it a question of fact.

In *USDAW v Leancut Bacon* (1981), the employer had spent six months trying to negotiate a take-over. The bidding company, however, pulled out after studying the employers half-yearly accounts, whereupon the employers bankers withdrew credit facilities and put in a receiver. Two days later, the employees were made redundant. In this case, the EAT considered that the employers could rely on the special circumstances defence.

Remedies

If the employer fails to comply with these requirements, a claim may be lodged with the industrial tribunal:

- in the case of a failure relating to elected representatives, by any of the employee representatives;
- in the case of a failure relating to a trade union representative by the trade union;
- in any other case, by any of the employees who have who have been or will be made redundant.

The claim must be presented either before the proposed dismissals take effect, or within three months of the dismissals, unless it was not 'reasonably practical' for it to do so.

If the claim is well-founded, the tribunal must make a declaration to that effect and may make a 'protective award' which will be for the protected period – that is a period beginning with the date on which the first dismissal complained of took place and lasting as long as the tribunal considers 'just and equitable'. This is subject to maximum periods which are 90 days where the minimum consultation period was 90 days, 30 days where the minimum consultation period was 30 days.

The protective award

In *Spillers French v USDAW* (1979), the EAT considered whether the protective award was intended to be compensatory or penal. Since the Act instructs the tribunal to take into consideration the seriousness of the employers fault, the EAT considered that it was not intended to be based entirely on the loss to the employee, and the fact that they had not suffered a loss did not mean that an award could not be made.

If the protective award is not paid by the employer, then the employee must complain to an industrial tribunal.

The Court of Appeal has recently confirmed that the tribunal has no power to order an injunction to prevent the dismissals.

However, in *R v British Coal, ex p Vardre* the court issued a declaration that no collieries were to be closed until the specified procedures have been followed.

Consultation under TUPE

'Long enough' before a 'relevant transfer', both transferor and transferee employers have a duty to consult appropriate representatives (see consultation on redundancies) of any affected employees.

They must be informed of:

• the fact of the transfer;
• the reasons for the transfer;
• the timing of the transfer;
• the legal, economic and social implications of the transfer.

Where the employers intend to take any measures which may affect their employees, they must consult the representatives about the measures; they must consider any representations made by the representatives; and they must give reasons if they reject those representations.

Note
Each employer only needs to consult his own representatives.

Defence

A similar defence of 'special circumstances' as with consultation on redundancies.

Remedies

As with redundancies (see above).
The tribunal may make a protective award of a 'just and equitable' sum of up to four weeks' pay.

Note
Under Regulation 9 if an undertaking or part of an undertaking is transferred and it retains its identity distinct from the remainder of the transferees business, then any recognition of a union is transferred. (It can however be de-recognised!)
If the identity is not preserved, Regulation 9 does not apply.
Under Regulation 6, any collective bargain agreed by the transferor is transferred to the transferee. (Note – collective bargains are not legally enforceable unless this is specifically stated in the agreement.)

Health and safety

Where a union is recognised, it is entitled to appoint safety representatives who have certain rights with regard to investigating potential hazards in the workplace, and employees complaints, and also conducting safety inspections. They must also be consulted by the employer on safety matters.

Pensions

If an employer wishes its employees to be contracted out of the state earnings related pension scheme, it must consult recognised independent trade unions, in default of which a contracting out certificate must be refused.

Works Councils

The European Works Council Directive, issued under the Social Chapter provides as follows:

- A European Works Council (EWC) or a procedure for informing and consulting employees must be established in every community-scale undertaking, ie undertakings with at least 1,000 employees in the European Union; and at least 150 in each of at least two Member States.

- The Central Management is responsible for implementing this obligation. Where it resides outside the EU, the obligation must be carried out by its representative agents.

- The management must set up a special negotiating body which is charged with determining with central management various matters concerning the EWC, including its scope, functions, composition and terms of office.

- The Directive does not apply if there is an information and consultation agreement covering the entire workforce already in operation.

- Subsidiary requirements must be laid down by the member state in which the central management is situated; and these will apply if the central management refuses to commence negotiations within six months of a request from employees; or if the parties fail to agree, within three years of such request.

These subsidiary arrangements should provide:

(a) the EWC should be composed of 3–30 employees.

(b) the EWC should have the right to meet with central management once a year to be informed and consulted on the progress of the business.

(c) the EWC also should have the right to be informed of any special event, eg relocation, closure or collective redundancies.

- Central management should not be obliged to transmit information which would seriously harm the undertaking and be prejudicial to the organisation.

- Members of special negotiating bodies should not be authorised to reveal any information where it has been expressly provided to them in confidence.

Now that the UK is to join the Social Chapter, measures will have to be taken to implement this Directive. However, the timescale for doing this is not yet available.

11 Trade unions and employers – industrial action

You should be familiar with the following areas:

* the common law liability for industrial action
* the immunities
* the loss of immunities
* the liability of trade unions
* the remedies for industrial action
* the law on picketing
* the 'right to strike'

There is no general right to strike in the UK, unlike many other countries where such a right is enshrined in their constitutions. You will have seen in Chapter 7 that it is automatically fair to dismiss an employee whilst he is on strike, provided that there is no victimisation; social security benefits are also withheld from strikers.

There is no general right for trade unions to organise a strike either. Trade unions ceased to be illegal organisations with the passing of the Trade Union Act 1871. The Conspiracy and Protection of Property Act 1876 further provided that anything done 'in contemplation or furtherance of a trade dispute' (the golden formula) was not a criminal conspiracy – unless the act itself was a crime. However, trade unions still found themselves in conflict with the civil law in *Taff Vale Rly v Amalgamated Society of Railway Servants* (1901) where the House of Lords held that the union must pay damages to the company for losses caused to it by a strike.

Following this, the government passed the Trade Disputes Act 1906 which gave trade unions total immunity from action in tort, and individuals, immunity from actions for conspiracy or inducing a breach of contract, provided they were acting 'in contemplation or furtherance of a trade dispute'. The statutory protection was extended to cover the tort of intimidation in 1965, following the case of *Rookes v Barnard* (below). This remained the position until 1971 when a different model was briefly introduced by the Industrial Relations Act which was itself repealed in 1974 with the previous situation being restored. Since 1980, however, there have been extensive changes, but the basic system of torts and immunities still remain. In order to establish the liability or otherwise of a trade union for any form of industrial action it is necessary:

- to identify the commission of a tort;
- to examine whether it is covered by a statutory immunity;
- to check whether the immunity has been lost;
- to explore the liability of trade unions;
- to identify the appropriate remedy.

This chapter follows that sequence in examining the liability of trade unions for organising industrial action.

Liability in tort

The economic torts normally involve deliberate action designed to cause economic loss to the plaintiff. Damages for economic loss is therefore recoverable because the loss is intentional. They are based on the illegal infliction of harm, rather than the unjustified infliction of harm.

Conspiracy

An agreement by two or more persons to do an unlawful act, or to do a lawful act by unlawful means.

Conspiracy to injure

This makes unlawful when done by two, what would be lawful if done by one. The predominant purpose of the action must be to injure the other party. If causing injury not promoting the unions interest is the main purpose, then the tort has been committed.

In *Quinn v Leatham* (1901) Leatham refused to dismiss non-unionists, but offered to pay their union fees. He was told that unless he dismissed them, his customers would be threatened with a strike if they continued to do business with him. Held: the tort of conspiracy had been committed. However, if the purpose is to further union interests, there is no conspiracy, as in *Crofter Hand-Woven Harris Tweeds v Veitch* (1942) where it was held that the unions action in 'blacking' the supplies of the plaintiff and other suppliers who were outside the 'closed shop' operated by the union, was legitimate as its object was to further the interest of the union and its members.

The anomalous nature of the tort has long been recognised; it has been detected very rarely, but the House of Lords stated in *Lonrho v Shell* (1982) that it was too well-established to be discarded.

Conspiracy to use unlawful means

There must be an intention to injure, but it need not be the predominant intention. This was established by the House of Lords in *Lonrho v Fayed* (1991).

'Unlawful means'

- They must be integral to the act – not, eg speeding to a meeting.
- Unlawful acts include crimes and torts and probably breaches of contract.
  Both branches of the tort require:

(a) two or more persons to be involved;

(b) a combination, ie a common purpose;

(c) damage suffered by the plaintiff.

The immunities (see below) cover a conspiracy to injure, but not a conspiracy to injure by unlawful means. However, actions which are covered by an immunity cannot amount to unlawful means, so if the tort which provides the unlawful means is covered by an immunity then it ceases to be unlawful..

Inducing a breach of contract

This tort is the one most commonly committed during a strike. The tort may be committed in one of two ways.

Direct inducement

This is committed when A persuades B to break his (Bs) contract with C. It was first established in *Lumley v Guy* (1853) where Guy persuaded a well-known soprano to break her contract with Lumley and to sing for him instead. It requires:

- a knowledge of the contract;
- an inducement to break the contract;
- an actual breach of contract.

It is committed when a union which is in dispute with an employer calls its members out on strike in breach of their contracts of employment with that employer.

Indirect inducement

This occurs when a trade union who is in dispute with firm A calls out on strike its members who work for firm B in order to effect a breach of a commercial contract between A and B. This is direct inducement of a breach of a contract of employment against firm B and an indirect inducement of a breach of a commercial contract against firm A.

For an indirect inducement to be a tort, unlawful methods must be used. The classic statement of the elements of the tort of indirectly inducing a breach of contract is found in the judgment of Jenkins LJ in *Thomson v Deakin* (1952) where the plaintiff was well known for not employing union members. The TGWU called on its members who drove for Bowaters to 'black' supplies to Thompson. Bowaters did not ask their drivers to deliver to Thompsons, but instead informed Thompson that they were unable to fulfil their contract.

He stipulated four requirements:

1 The defendant knew of the existence of the contract and intended to procure its breach. Originally, actual knowledge of the contracts terms was required, but more recently the courts have interpreted this requirement more broadly, and it is not necessary to know the precise terms of the contract, only that the contract existed.

In *Merkur Island Shipping Co Ltd v Laughton* (1983), a union had blacked a ship in Liverpool docks. The House of Lords held that the union must have known of the existence of commercial contracts which would be broken if the fully-laden ships could not leave port and this was sufficient.

Similarly, the requirement for intention has been extended to cover a reckless indifference as to whether the contract would be terminated lawfully or not. In *Emerald Construction v Lothian* (1966), the union wished to rid a building site of Emerald who were labour only subcontractors. Such sub-contractors normally were entitled to very short periods of notice, but Emerald was entitled to an unusually long period. The union called a strike to force the main contractors to get rid of Emerald. It was held that the union wanted the contract terminated, lawfully or unlawfully. It had deliberately turned a blind eye to the specific terms and wanted Emerald out.

2 The defendants persuaded or procured employees to break their contracts of employment with this intention.

It is sometimes difficult to distinguish between persuasion and communicating information. A statement of fact was held not to be an inducement in *Thomson v Deakin* where it was held that an inducement involved 'pressure, persuasion or procuration' but the courts have again broadened their view. It has been suggested that if information is communicated with the intention that it should bring about a breach, then it is inducement; and the fact that it is described as information or advice or a friendly warning will not alter the situation.

3 The employees did break their contracts of employment.

4 A breach of a commercial contract ensued as a necessary consequence of the breach of the contracts of employment. (But see *Torquay Hotel Co Ltd v Cousins* (1969).)

Notes 3 and 4 are factual matters. Did the inducement lead to the workers breaking their contracts of employment? Did that lead as a necessary consequence to the breach of the commercial contract? The answer will depend on the facts of each particular case.

In the case of indirect inducement, 'unlawful means' are required. For example a breach of contract, a tort, or some other form of civil liability, eg a breach of statutory duty.

It was held in *Meade v Haringey Council* (1979) that inducing a local authority to break its statutory duty to provide education was a tort. (It should be noted that the statutory immunity covers breach of contract but not breach of statutory duty.)

Who can sue?
The limits of the remoteness rule is not totally clear, eg:

• Employers who have suffered breaches of contracts of employment can sue.

• Persons who suffer a breach of a commercial contract where the breach was intended can sue.

• It is not clear whether other persons who have suffered a breach of a commercial contract but who were not the intended objects of the action can sue.

In *Falconer v ASLEF* (1986) a commuter successfully sued the union in a county court for expenses incurred as a result of a strike, on the ground that the union must have intended to inconvenience him as this was a way of putting pressure on British Rail.

However, in *Barretts & Baird v IPS* (1987) where abattoirs were unable to operate due to a strike by meat inspectors, the court held that it was an essential element of the tort that the unions predominate purpose should have been to harm the plaintiffs, and the action therefore failed (see Citizens Charter below).

Defences
There is a possible defence of justification, but it has only been successful in one case. See *Brimelow v Casson* (1924); *SW Miners Federation v Glamorgan Coal Co Ltd* (1905).

Interference with a contract

A new tort of interfering with a contract was discovered in *Torquay Hotel Co v Cousins* (1969). The TGWU were in dispute with the hotel owners who refused to recognise the union. The union informed Esso that a particular hotel was blacked and that fuel supplies to it should stop. Esso, most of whose drivers belonged to the TGWU made no attempt to deliver oil to the hotel. There was a *force majeure* clause in the contract with the hotel, so they were not liable for breach of contract. The Court of Appeal were uncertain as to whether there was a breach of contract which was excused or whether the *force majeure* clause prevented there being a breach at all. However they held that this did not matter, as it was also a tort to interfere with a contract. This was confirmed as a tort by the House of Lords in *Merkur Island Shipping v Laughton*.

Intimidation

This was introduced by the House of Lords in *Rookes v Barnard* (1964) Barnard, the branch secretary of the union which operated a closed shop at BOAC, told the company that if they did not dismiss Rookes who had resigned from the union, they would organise a strike. Rookes was consequently dismissed with the requisite notice, so there was no breach of contract. Rookes sued on the basis that the threat of a strike (a breach of contract) was a threat of an unlawful act. The House of Lords agreed that the threat of a breach of contract was an unlawful threat for the purpose of intimidation.

This was a very controversial decision:

- Prior to this case, it had been thought that a threat of physical violence was required for the tort of intimidation, *cf*: duress in contract.
- The plaintiff was dismissed lawfully with notice.
- There was no breach of contract by the employees; if they had gone on strike the immunities would have applied.
- The defendant was a union official, not an employee; he could not have threatened a breach of contract.

The requirements of the tort

1 The defendant must threaten the third party or pressurise him into a course of action.
2 The threat must be of some unlawful act, such as crime, tort, or breach of contract.
3 The threatened person must submit to the threat.
4 The plaintiff must suffer damage.

Interference with trade or business by unlawful means

It has been suggested that the above nominate torts should be drawn together into one innominate tort – interfering with trade or business by unlawful means. In 1906, this was protected by an immunity. However, in 1982, this immunity was repealed on the ground that it was unnecessary.

It is argued:

- if there had been an immunity, there must have been a tort;
- if there is a tort of 'intimidation', ie threatening to use unlawful means to interfere with a business. then there must be a tort of interfering with a business by unlawful means;
- the tort was referred to by Lord Denning in *Torquay Hotel v Cousin* and recognised by the House of Lords in *Merkur v Laughton* and in *Lonrho v Fayed* (1989).

'Unlawful means' could be:

- the commission of a tort (other than one protected by an immunity);
- a breach of contract, or threat to break a contract (*Rookes v Barnard*);
- a breach of a statutory duty (*Meade v Haringey LBC* (1979) and *Assoc British Ports v TGWU* (1989)).

- contempt of court;
- a crime – not necessarily. In *Lonrho v Shell* it was pointed out that not every statute creating an offence also created the tort of breach of a statutory duty.

Other possible torts

Economic duress
See *Universe Tankship v ITF* (1982). This would be an unjustified infliction of injury rather than an illegal one.

Inducing a breach of a statutory duty
See *Meade v Haringey* (1979); *Assoc British Ports v TGWU* (1989).

Immunity under TULR(C)A 1992

Section 219 gives immunity from action for the torts of:
- inducing a breach of contract;
- interfering with a contract by unlawful means;
- threatening to do either;
- conspiracy, providing the act done by one person alone would not be actionable.

There is no immunity for interfering with trade or business by unlawful means, or conspiracy by unlawful means, but actions covered by an immunity do not amount to unlawful means provided the tort is committed 'in contemplation or furtherance of a trade dispute'.

A 'trade dispute' is defined in s 244(1) of the TULR(C)A as a dispute between workers and their employer which relates wholly or mainly to one of the following:
- terms and conditions of employment, or the physical conditions in which any worker is required to work;
- engagement or non-engagement, or termination or suspension of employment or the duties of employment, of one or more workers;
- allocation of work or the duties of employment between workers or groups of workers;
- matters of discipline;
- a worker's membership or non-membership of a trade union;
- facilities for officials of trade unions; and

- machinery for negotiation, and other procedures relating to any of the above matters, including the recognition by employers or employers associations of the rights of a trade union to represent workers in such negotiation or consultation or in the carrying out of such procedures.

Note

- There must be a dispute. In *Brent v Hogan* (1945) a union asked brewery managers for confidential information regarding income in order to frame a pay claim. It was not protected by the immunities when sued for inducing a breach of contract (the implied term of confidentiality) as there was no dispute at that time.

- Between 'workers and their employers' (pre-1982 the wording included disputes between 'workers and workers' and 'workers and employers'). In *Dimbleby & Sons Ltd v NUJ* (1984), journalists employed by Dimbleby refused to send copy to TBF Ltd, rather than to their own associated printing house, T Bailey Foreman, where the printers were on strike. TBF Ltd was also an associate company of T Bailey Foreman. The journalists were taking sympathy action to support the printers. The NUJ first argued that they were employed by the same employer, and second that the dispute was about the allocation of work. While the House of Lords accepted that the dispute was about the allocation of work, the journalists were not in dispute with their employer. All the companies were separate legal entities, and the journalists were not employed by T Bailey Foreman who was the employer in dispute.

- For a proper purpose, ie not for a political purpose.

In *BBC v Hearn* (1977), the union asked its members not to transmit the Cup Final after the BBC had refused to take steps to see that the broadcast would not be transmitted to South Africa, whose policy of apartheid the union opposed. Held: there was not trade dispute but a political dispute which was not covered by the immunities. (Lord Denning suggested that had the union asked for a clause to be inserted in the staffs contract allowing them to be dictated by their conscience in such matters, this would have been turned into a trade dispute. This was subsequently disapproved of by the House of Lords.)

Note

Since 1982, the dispute must relate 'wholly or mainly' to the trade dispute, not merely be 'connected with' it.

In *Mercury Communications Ltd v Scott Garner* (1984), a dispute arose out of the government's licensing of operators other than British Telecom to operate telecommunications. The POEU instructed its members employed by BT not to connect Mercury, a private company to the BT network. The union argued that it had issued this instruction in furtherance of a dispute with BT over employees job security, which it claimed would be put at risk if Mercury was connected. The Court of Appeal rejected this argument, and held that the dispute was primarily concerned with the union's objection to government policy. In reaching this decision, the court was heavily influenced by evidence of a Job Security Agreement between the union and the employer, which the union had not sought to invoke, a fact which pointed away from the union having a genuine concern about jobs.

However in *Wandsworth LBC v NAS/NUT* (1994) where the union had instructed its members to boycott all unreasonable and unnecessary elements of the national curriculum, the Court of Appeal rejected the councils claim that the boycott was motivated by ideological objection to the tests and accepted that it was about teachers working time, and was therefore mainly related to the terms and conditions of employment. The court paid considerable importance to the ballot which preceded the industrial action which asked the members whether they were willing to take industrial action 'to protest about the excessive workload and unreasonable imposition made on teachers by the national curriculum and assessment and testing'. See also *Assoc British Ports v TGWU* (1989).

- Which affects workers in this country. (The union in *BBC v Hearn* would now also fail on this ground.)

The dispute must be 'in contemplation or furtherance of' the trade dispute. In a number of cases in the 1970s, the Court of Appeal under Lord Denning tried to develop a doctrine of 'remoteness', and to remove immunity from activities they considered too removed from the original dispute, ie secondary action, which was used with considerable effect during the 'winter of discontent'. However, the House of Lords held that 'acting in contemplation or furtherance' was to be judged objectively. As long as a person genuinely believed that it assisted in achieving the objectives, then he was acting 'in contemplation or furtherance of a trade dispute', even if the belief was an irrational one.

In *Express Newspapers v McShane* (1980), the NUJ was in dispute with provincial newspapers. Their members came out on strike but the strike was ineffective as the newspapers still obtained news from the

Press Association. The union then called out their members at the Press Association, but many ignored the call to strike. The union then called upon their members in the National Newspapers to 'black' news from the Press Association. Lord Denning and the Court of Appeal decided that this action was too remote from the original dispute and unlikely to have any effect on it and was therefore not 'in contemplation or furtherance of a trade dispute'. The decision was overturned by the House of Lords for the above reasons.

In *Duport Steel v Sirs* (1980), after British Steel refused a pay claim the steel unions called their members out on strike. As this had very little effect, they then called out their members in the private steel companies in order to put pressure on the government to intercede and make more money available to the Corporation. Again Lord Denning held that the strike in the private sector was too remote from the original dispute with British Steel and that in fact it was in pursuance of their dispute with the government. Again, the decision was reversed by the House of Lords who held that it was in contemplation or furtherance of a trade dispute.

Loss of immunities

The above immunities will be lost in the following situations.

A Secondary action

Section 224 of the TULR(C)A 1992 removes immunity for inducing a breach of, or interfering with a contract of employment, or threatening to do so, where the employer under the contract of employment is not a party to the dispute; except in the case of lawful picketing (see below). A contract of employment for these purposes, includes work done by an independent contractor who undertakes to do the work personally.

B Action for prohibited purpose

Section 224 of the TULR(C)A 1992 will not be a defence in the following circumstances:

- Industrial action taken to put pressure on an employer to impose union membership and union recognition requirements, eg in a closed shop (ss 144–45 and 186–87 of the TULR(C)A 1992) also renders void any terms in a contract which requires the other party to recognise a trade union or to maintain a closed shop).

- Sections 222–25 of the TULR(C)A 1992 provide that there will be no immunity for industrial action designed to get such terms inserted into contracts between employers.

- Pressure to maintain a closed shop. Section 222 of the TULR(C)A 1992 removes immunity 'if one of the reasons was to pressurise the employer to discriminate against non-union members'.

- Reinstatement of strikers. Section 223 of the TULR(C)A 1992 removes immunity from industrial action which is even partly taken because of the dismissals of unofficial strikers.

C Failure to hold a ballot

Immunity from the tort of inducing a breach of contract, or interfering with its performance will be lost, unless a ballot is held in advance of the action (but not threatening a breach of contract, ie intimidation).

This only applies to 'official' strikes. Immunity is not lost in this way in the case of unofficial strikes.

Note
Any union member has a right to restrain a trade union from calling for industrial action without a ballot. Normally, an employer must await the industrial action to start before he can take action.

However, in *P & O Ferries v NUS* (1988) an injunction was awarded to stop the union balloting on secondary action.

Requirements of a valid ballot
(See also Code of Practice on Trade Union Ballots.)

- It must be a postal ballot.

- Only those who are thought reasonably likely to take part in the industrial action should be balloted. Standard – reasonable practicability. It was held in *BRB v ITT* (1985) that a ballot is not invalid because a few members did not receive a ballot paper.

In *London Underground Ltd v NURMTW* (1995), the union had organised a ballot of its members and this had resulted in a vote in favour of industrial action. The union served the requisite notice on the employers and included the names of 20 new members who had joined the union after the ballot. It then served notice of further industrial action and this included the names of a further 672 employees who had joined the union since the strike and had not been included in the first notice. The employers alleged that since a large number of new members had been included the action could not be said to be supported by a ballot, and sought an injunction. The Court of Appeal held that industrial action is to be regarded as having the support of a ballot if a majority of those voting have declared themselves willing to take part. The participation of a particular individual in collective industrial action, and the industrial action itself are two different things. It is the industrial action which must have the support of the ballot, not the participation of those taking part in it. The view expressed *obiter* by Lord Donaldson in *PO v UCW* (1990) that 'any call for industrial action following a ballot should be limited to those who were given an opportunity to vote' was unsustainable in so far as it related to changes in union membership.

- Where there are separate workplaces, then if all members are balloted (or all members in the same bargaining unit) separate returns are not needed, but if a union is planning to ballot only some of its members at different workplaces, and cannot justify this on neutral grounds – separate ballots must be organised.

A ballot may be held covering employees of different employers if it is reasonable for the union to believe that there are common factors (*University of Central England v NALGO* (1993)).

- The ballot paper

  (a) Must contain the statement 'If you take part in the strike, or other appropriate course of action, you may be in breach of your contract of employment' (health warning) even in the case of an overtime ban.

  (b) If industrial action short of a strike is contemplated, as well as a strike, then the two questions must be placed separately. In *PO v UCW* (1990), the union asked members if they would be prepared to take industrial action up to and including 'strike action'. The Court of Appeal held that this rolled up question did not comply with the requirements, and rendered the ballot ineffective.

  In *West Midlands Travel Ltd v TGWU* (1994), the Court of Appeal decided that where a union holds a ballot on industrial action, and more than one question appears on the ballot paper, then for the purpose of counting votes each question is to be effectively treated as a separate ballot. It is sufficient, therefore, for the majority of those voting on a particular question to have said 'yes' to action, even if they do not constitute a majority of those who had returned ballot papers. (Q.1 – 1,265 – yes; 1,225 – no; 147 – blank: Q.2 – 1,059 – yes; 1,156 – no; 427 – blank. 2,642 members had voted altogether. The employer sued the TGWU for damages to cover their loss of £419,000.)

In *London Borough of Newham v NALGO* (1993), the Court of Appeal confirmed that the union was perfectly entitled to be partisan. In that case, the voting paper asked whether the members were prepared to go on strike, 'on strike pay equivalent to full take home pay'.

(c) Must contain a statement of who is to call legal action.

In *Tanks and Drums v TGWU* (1991) the union had nominated its general secretary as having authority to call a strike. Negotiations with the employer had been led by the union's district secretary. Two weeks after the ballot in favour, the district official obtained the general secretary's permission to implement the action if a better offer was not forthcoming after a meeting with the employer the next day. As no further offer was made the strike went ahead. The employer sued for an interim injunction claiming that the general secretary had delegated his power to decide. The Court held that this was not a blanket delegation; the permission was specific enough to warrant holding that the general secretary had called the action as required by the legislation.

- A scrutineer must be appointed (unless under 50 are entitled to vote).
- Notice must be given to the employer:
  (a) seven days before opening of ballot, giving date of ballot, describing (so that they can be easily identified) the members likely to vote;
  (b) three days before the ballot, giving a specimen ballot paper;
  (c) seven days before industrial action, to employers of members likely to take part stating whether the action is intended to be continuous or discontinuous, and describing (so that he may readily ascertain them) the members likely to take part.

In *Blackpool & Fylde College v NATFE* (1994), the union gave the requisite notice to the employer which specified 'all our members in your institution'. The employers argued that this was not sufficiently precise to enable it to identify those employees. The college had been told by the union previously that about a third of employees were union members (288), but only 109 had their dues debited from their salaries. The Court of Appeal thought it 'inescapable' that on these facts the employer had not received adequate information. The court was at pains to insist that unions would not necessarily be ordered to give names in every case, but where the union does not have 100% membership in a particular category, this is presumably what it means.

• Result

Bare majority of those voting sufficient.

(Note – voting now seen as valuable tactic by the union.)

• Timescale

Action must normally be called and must start within four weeks. In *RJB Mining v NUM* (1995), a ballot called by the union closed at 10 am Tuesday 16 May. The union called a series of one day strikes to commence with the day shift on Tuesday 16 June. It was held that the four-week period ended on midnight 15 June and an injunction was therefore issued. The Court of Appeal turned down the unions contention that since the day shift commenced at midnight on the 12/13 June, the action was within the four-week period. The court stated that the period finished at the end of one day and did not overlap into the next. Although 'midnight' is the word used to identify the end of one period and the beginning of another, it does not follow that there is a moment in time which belongs to both days. *Cf Monsanto v TGWU* (1987) where union members voted in favour of industrial action over the employment of temporary labour. The company responded with counter-sanctions, including the suspension of sick pay schemes, guaranteed week and early retirement schemes. The union suspended industrial action pending further sanctions, but reimposed it two weeks later after negotiations broke down. The Court of Appeal held that there was no need for a further ballot; the industrial action had not been discontinued but merely suspended temporarily for the purpose of negotiation with the employer, with the intention that it would be reimposed should the negotiations fail. The court also rejected that to reimpose action fell outside the terms of the ballot; these were sufficiently wide to encompass any matters within the scope of settling the original dispute.

In *PO v UCW* (1990), however, the Court of Appeal held that a ballot in September 1988, did not render lawful a strike in September

1989, although there had been industrial conflict in the meantime, ie a series of selective 24-hour strikes between October and December, culminating in a national one-day strike in December. There was no action between January and April 1989, but in May action started again, culminating in a strike in September. The disputes were all over the same issue, but the Court of Appeal held that the dispute which began in May was a new campaign and that a fresh ballot should have taken place before the action commenced.

It has been suggested that where industrial action is suspended, the union should make clear to their members that this is contingent on the successful outcome of negotiations; and that it is important to ensure that the terms of the questions on the ballot paper are wide enough to cover any matter which might arise out of the dispute.

Note
Where an interlocutory injunction is issued the union may call for an extension of time.

The balloting arrangements are extremely complicated and detailed and it has been argued that a trade union which wishes to comply with the law finds it very difficult to know how to do so.

New union liability (Citizens Right of Action)

Application to the court by members of the public is allowed for unlawful industrial action which is likely to prevent or delay the supply of goods or services to them, or reduce their quality.

The remedy is an injunction.

A commissioner for protection against unlawful industrial action
See Chapter 1, p 11.

Liability of the trade union

Trade unions are now protected against actions in tort, only if they are acting in 'contemplation or furtherance of a trade dispute'. Section 22 of the TULR(C)A 1992 now provides that a trade union will only be liable if the act in question is authorised or endorsed by a responsible person of the union. For example:

- the principle executive committee;
- any other person empowered by the rules to authorise or endorse the kind of act in question;
- the president or general secretary;
- any official, whether or not employed by the union, or any committee;

  An act will be that of an official if it is done by any group of which he is a member.
- any committee of the union to whom an employed official regularly reports.

Note

A trade union may repudiate the acts in question through its executive committee, president, or general secretary, provided they do so at the earliest opportunity, and they do not act in a manner that is inconsistent with the repudiation.

Written notice must be given to the committee or individual involved, also to strikers and the employer and must contain a stipulated statement.

Financial limits

If a trade union is successfully sued in tort, there are limits to the amount of damages which may be awarded, dependent on the size of the union's membership:

Under 5,000 members –	£10,000 limit
Between 5,000–25,000 –	£50,000 limit
Between 25,000–100,000 –	£125,000 limit
Over 100,000 members –	£250,000 limit

Remedies

1 Damages

   See limits on liability of trade unions.
2 Injunctions

   The most common remedy sought is an interlocutory injunction.

   In *American Cynamid Co v Ethicon Ltd* (1975), the court laid down the following tests for the issue of an interlocutory injunction.

(a) Is there a serious issue to be tried?

(b) Has the plaintiff shown that the action if continued would do him irreparable harm which cannot be remedied by a subsequent award of damages?

(c) On the balance of convenience is the harm suffered by the plaintiff greater than the harm which would be suffered by the defendant if he had to cease his action.

Section 221 of the TULR(C)A 1992 provides that:

- If there might be a trade dispute defence to the request, the court should not grant an injunction *ex parte* until all reasonable steps have been taken to inform the defendant, and give him an opportunity to state his case.
- The court must have regard to the fact that the defendant might succeed in a trade dispute defence at a full trial.

In *NWL v Woods* (1979) it was stated by the court that if it is likely that the defence would succeed at a full trial, then an injunction should not be ordered.

The legal consequences of breaching an injunction:

1 Committal for contempt of court.

2 Sequestration.

Picketing

The term picketing is used to describe the conduct of persons who seek to persuade other persons to take a certain course of action, or not to do something, usually entering work premises or delivering supplies during industrial action.

Three main problems exist with regard to picketing:

(a) It is unclear whether the simple act of picketing is unlawful or not.

(b) There is no clear distinction between picketing and public demonstration.

(c) Whereas the law gives protection only for 'peaceful communication or persuasion', pickets often see their object as stopping people from working.

Section 15(1) of the TULR(C)A 1992 says:

'It shall be lawful for a person in contemplation or furtherance of a trade dispute to attend:

(a) his own place of work; or

(b) if he is an official of a trade union, at or near the place of work of a member of that union whom he is accompanying and whom he represents, for the purpose only of peacefully obtaining or communicating information, or peacefully persuading any person to work or abstain from working' (cf 'secondary action').

There are three exceptions to 'own place of work' requirement.

• If workers work normally at more than one place of work, or it is impracticable to picket their own place of work, then they may picket the place from where their work is administered.

• Workers who are dismissed during the dispute in question may picket their former place of work. But see *News Group Newspapers v SOGAT* (1986) where it was held that employees dismissed when News International moved from Fleet Street to Wapping were not entitled to picket at Wapping, because they had never worked there.

• Trade union officials (see above).

For 'near' see *Rayware Ltd v TGWU* (1989).

• See also the Code of Practice on picketing; in particular the advice that six pickets should be the optimum number and which has been applied by the courts to such an extent that it is now almost seen as the law.

Civil liability for picketing

1 The economic torts

For example, interfering with a contract, etc.

In *Union Traffic Ltd v TGWU* (1989), the Court of Appeal held that the mere presence of pickets may be deemed sufficient to constitute an 'inducement', if it clear that their presence is intended to induce a breach of contract. (It must however be directed at one of the parties to the dispute – *Middlebrook Mushrooms v TGWU* (1993).)

2 Private nuisance

That is unlawful interference with a person's enjoyment or use of his own land. In *News Group Newspapers v SOGAT* (1986), it was held that the behaviour of the pickets or demonstrators did interfere with the right of the plaintiff to enjoy his own property, as he had to incur extra transport and security costs, and also suffered a high turnover of staff as a result of the action.

In *Thomas v NUM (South Wales Area)* (1986), the High Court held that:

- mass picketing in itself constituted a nuisance;
- regular picketing outside the home of a non-striker would constitute a private nuisance;
- interference by harassment of employees who wished to go to work was a species of private nuisance (since doubted) and also an unreasonable interference with a persons right to use the highway;
- the daily presence of 50/70 men hurling abuse, requiring the presence of the police, and the use of vehicles to transport employees to work amounted to a nuisance.

Does peaceful picketing amount to private nuisance, when not protected by the formula? In *Hubbard v Pitt* (1976), Lord Denning stated 'picketing by itself is not a nuisance', but Lord Justice Orr stated that the picketers state of mind was important, and in this case he was satisfied that the picketers intended to interfere with the plaintiffs business.

In *Thomas v NUM* (1986), Scott J stated that picketing by itself would not amount to common law nuisance, but held that it would be tortious if it interfered with the plaintiffs right to use the highway; and in that case the injunction granted by the court restricted picketing to peacefully communicating information in numbers not exceeding six.

3   Public nuisance

In *News Group Newspapers v SOGAT* (1986) the conduct of the pickets and demonstrators was found to be an unreasonable use of the highway, and the plaintiff was found to have suffered special damage (see also *Thomas v NUM* (1986)).

4   Trespass

To mount a picket on the employers land would be tortious.

Criminal liability

It is the criminal law which is of the greatest practical significance, eg during the miners' strike over 11,000 criminal charges were brought.

The immunity given by TULR(C)A is no defence to a criminal charge.

Breach of the peace

Obstructing a police officer in the course of his duty.

Police have wide discretion. A policeman has a duty to prevent a breach of the peace. If a police officer believes that a breach of the peace is about to be committed, he has a duty to prevent it. Resistance would be an offence.

In *Piddington v Bates* (1961) a policeman ordered the pickets to be reduced to two. The defendant pushed past the policeman with the statement that he knew his rights. He was arrested charges with obstruction and found guilty.

The refusal of a police order to stop obstructing the highway was an offence in *Tynan Balmer* (1967).

In *Broome v McLachlan* (1985), it was held that the police have a power to disperse pickets some way from their destination if they reasonably believe a breach of the peace will occur should they get to their destination. In that case pickets from Kent were stopped on the M1 before they could reach Nottinghamshire.

Obstruction of the highway

Pickets have no right to stop a vehicle if they do not wish to stop. In *Broome v DPP* (1974), a picket failed to persuade a lorry driver to stop, and thereafter stood in front of the lorry, and refused to move when asked to do so by the police. The House of Lords held that there was no right to obstruct the highway, only a freedom, and the picket should have been convicted of obstruction.

Public nuisance

It is an offence to obstruct the public in the exercise of their right to free passage along the highway (s 241 of the TULR(C)A 1992 – originally in The Conspiracy and Protection of Property Act 1875).

The following offences are committed by those who try to compel another to do or not do something:

- using violence towards or intimidating that person, his family, or injuring his property;
- persistently following that person from place to place;
- hiding tools, clothes or other property, or depriving or hindering the use of such;
- watching or besetting the persons home, workplace, or the approach to either;
- following a person with two or more others in a disorderly fashion in any road or street.

Watching and besetting is the most common charge, but it must be done wrongfully and without legal authority. Thus if the picket is covered by an immunity, it will not be wrongful unless some other wrong has been committed (*Thomas v NUM*).

Public Order Act 1994

In particular, note:

Part 1: s 1 – riot; s 2 – violent disorder; s 3 – affray; s 4 – causing fear, or provoking violence; s 4 – causing harassment, alarm, or distress.

Part 2: ss 11–13 – police must be given advance notice of processions and can impose conditions if they think it necessary to prevent serious disorder or damage to property or disruption to the life of the community; s 14 – conditions may be imposed on any public assembly on the same grounds.

A 'right to strike'

There has been considerable discussion in recent years as to whether the immunities which protect trade unions in certain circumstances should be replaced by a 'right to strike' as is the case in many other European countries. In the early 1980s, the CBI and other employer organisations promoted the move to a closely defined 'right to strike' as a means of limiting the industrial power of trade unions. It has since been seen that this can be done by limiting the immunities, and the enthusiasm for a 'right to strike' is now seen as a way to remove 'the insecure foundation of the freedom to strike'.

The reason for the development of immunities rather than a 'right' is explained by Lord Wedderburn as lying in the history of working class movements in this country. Trade unions were comparatively strong at an early date, before there was a working class political party, or indeed universal franchise. The 'right' in other European countries developed out of ideological movement which often preceded strong trade unions. Secondly, 'rights' are not a feature of the British Constitution which in any case is 'unwritten'. There is no 'right' to free speech either.

Arguments for a 'right to strike'

- Immunities protect only the organisers of strikes.

At common law, a strike is a fundamental breach of contract which allows the striker to be *summarily dismissed*.

Under unfair dismissal provisions, it is automatically fair to dismiss a striker, provided there is no victimisation; but even victimisation is allowed in the case of an unofficial strike.

This is contrasted with the position in France, Germany and Italy, where a strike does not involve a breach of contract, but a suspension of the contract.

• It would be an opportunity to simplify the system.

The present system is seen as unnecessarily complicated. There is the initial problem of understanding the economic torts; the scope of the immunities, the complicated provisions where the immunities are lost, and the responsibility of trade unions. The International Labour Organisation has complained about the complexity of English law in this area.

• 'Rights' would avoid the problem of courts developing new torts which are not covered by existing immunities.

For example, *Rookes v Barnard*; *Torquay Hotel v Cousins*; *Meade v Haringey*; *Merkur Island Shipping v Laughton* (above).

• There is a problem with terminology in the present system. 'Immunities' are seen as social privileges not available to the rest of the community. Hayek declared: 'There will be no salvation for Britain until the special privileges granted to trade unions three-quarters of a century ago are revoked.'

Arguments against a change

• Kahn-Freund has pointed out that however the right is phrased there will still be a need for some limitations, eg strikes which harm outsiders, involve continuous processes, or essential services.

• Lord Wedderburn has pointed out that changing terminology will not get rid of problems. He has shown that the right to strike means different things in different European countries.

For example, in France and Italy, a 'strike' covers only a total cessation of work; but in Germany a 'work to rule' is also covered.

Most European countries give some protection to secondary action but the degree of protection differs.

In Germany the 'right to strike' has been reduced to a narrow range of circumstances by official trade unions alone, and then only when all procedures have been exhausted.

Considerable emphasis is placed in Europe on differences between conflicts of interest and conflicts of rights.

Lord Wedderburn stresses that in switching to a system based on 'rights' many decisions would have to be taken on a number of issues, and also that positive rights do not necessarily afford a wider area of industrial legality.

- 'Rights' would still be open to judicial interpretation. They would not avoid the hostility of the courts, eg:

    (a) picketing is already expressed as a right, but it is narrowly interpreted by the courts;

    (b) 'in contemplation or furtherance of a strike' was narrowly interpreted by the Court of Appeal in *Express Newspapers v McShane* and *Dupont Steels v Sirs*.

- One of the most intractable problems with regard to industrial action is the issuing of interlocutory injunctions. This would not be changed by reformulating the protection. Courts insist on the discretionary nature of injunctions.

- Several problems would be posed, eg:

    (a) 'no strike agreements' – could a 'right to strike' be negotiated away by trade unions?

    (b) will a 'right to strike' also extend to cover a 'right not to strike' Will protection be given against disciplinary action by trade unions or fellow employees?

    (c) will the 'right to strike' cover a 'right to lockout'?

Professor Ewing proposes that in addition to changing to a system based on rights, dismissal during a strike should be made automatically fair; and changes should be made to the granting of injunctions. Lord Wedderburn points out that the change from immunities to 'positive rights' solve few problems, but also create new problems. He suggests that the economic torts should be abolished, a labour court created, and that in a strike, the contract of employment should be suspended not breached.

'Rights' in most European countries have arisen out of their own historical development, as immunities have arisen out of the historical development in this country. However, the present government has intimated that they intend to incorporate the European Declaration of Human Rights into English law, so it may be that a right to withhold labour will become part of UK law.

Index